THE MARGRAVE FAMILY

COOKBOOK........

a northern exposure

For: Kelly, Phil, Julian and Ella - Bon Appetit!
J.K. Margrave

WRITTEN AND EDITED BY

Judith k. Margrave

Art work by Kella Marnon
Design and publishing arrangements by Sara E. Leeland
Sara Leeland Books   www.saraleelandbooks.net

Dedication

For my mother and father, Dorothy and Charles Margrave,
who taught me the meaning of good food.

For my cousin, Margo Boardwell, my best gal pal, who is
in her own right an excellent cook and
who encouraged me through the two years involved
in making this book.

For Sara Van Raalte Leeland, who believed in me.

Thoughts

Late November's wrath had hit hard in Michigan and I was sitting watching the flakes of white snow circle to the brown earth as I mindlessly looked for something constructive to do. Since I trip over my ego daily, this day was no different. I wanted a landmark by which I could be remembered and that would extend to future generations.

The 'landmark' would have something to do with food, since the marking thereof has been one of my passions since I first wrapped my little hand around my first cooking spoon. Aha! Collected recipes from a lifetime of gathering from my mother's friends and my friends; from former students, clips and snips from old newspapers and magazines and, of course, my food heroes of today. From all these sources came many beloved ideas for the making of culinary delights.

Some of the recipes were favorites of mine and my sons, Hal and Jarl Brey. We would look forward to holidays so that some of the more ethnic foods could surface and be shared with friends and family. As I began a two-year adventure of gathering, placing recipes in proper chapters and typing them on my computer, I laughed, cried and remembered the wonderful people who had shared their recipes with a struggling young cook—or former students who shared my passion for the culinary arts.

Some of the recipes are extremely easy and others are more challenging, but the effort is well worth the reward.

Please remember that many of these little gems are years and years old and, therefore, do not lend themselves to healthy eating. Do substitute ingredients if you choose.

Cooking is a handed-down legacy... so be it! Therefore, with lots and lots of love, I pass these recipes to my sons, Hal and Jarl Brey; to my four grandchildren, Elyse, Charlie, Mackenzie and Parker Brey; to my brother, Mack Margrave; my cousins, Margo Boardwell and her children, Deborah, Cynthia and Douglas; to Penny Munroe and her children, Kelly and Lee; and finally, to Charles Margrave (Nick) Nichols and his three sons, Carl, Chris and Jeff.

My hope is that they all will pass this Margrave book on to their children, and they onto theirs, so that the fun and creativeness of cooking will last forever and ever.

—Judith Kathryn Margrave

ANCESTRY

The Mormons were of real help in discovering my mother's family since she was adopted when she was but three days old. I located her birth certificate, tucked away in some of her belongings, and the Mormons helped me from that point. Her family was Irish and farmed; like many of the Irish, her family wisely set sail for America during the potato famine. I have gone back in time as much as I could to give this to you. I was privileged and blessed to travel to Ireland in 2008, setting for on the soil of County Tippeary, burying mom's little plaid hat while I wept. It was a very emotional experience for me since mom loved her Irish heritage. Being Irish and St. Patrick's Day, I had brought some of herself home. The O'Mearas are many in County Tipperary and I too had come home.

Judith Kathryn Margrave's Maternal Tree

Hugh O'Meara B. 1802 Ireland

Patrick Joseph O'Meara B 1826, Ireland   M.   Margaret Morris B. 1836, Canada

John, Margaret 1859, Anna 1860, Maria 1862; Michael Patrick 1863; Bridget 1866; Katherine 1868, Frank 1873; Hugh 1876; Edward Dennis 1879

Frank O'Meara 1873   M   Mabel Bard 1879

Madeline 1898; William 1899; Marguerite 1900; Kathlene 1913; Frances, William, Edward

Madeline 1898

Dorothy Margaret O'Meara 1916 (Robarge – Adoptive parents, Homer and Evelyn)

Dorothy Margaret Robarge B. 1916   M.   Charles Vincent Dean Margrave 1909

Judith Kathryn 1937;   John Mack Ramsey   M. Mary Hunt

Judith Kathryn 1937   M   Harold Dean Brey 1936

Harold Dean, Jr. 1959 : Jarl Joseph 1962

Harold Dean, Jr.   M   Debra Jeanne Hiss 1958

Jarl Joseph1962   M   Amy Upjohn 1961

Elizabeth Kathryn 1990; Charles Burton Harold 1992

M. Laura Hughson 1970

Mackenzie Jo 2000; Parker Robert 2002

JUDITH KATHRYN MARGRAVE'S PATERNAL TREE

Charlemagne Jerome Margrave (Nephew of the Ninth Duke of Argyle)   M.   Catherine De Hergusville

Twins, George and Frieda B. 1862, Aberdeen, Scotland

George Margrave 1862   M   Lucy Dean 1882

Marguerite Argyle - 1902; Lorna Dean – 1903; Audrey Alicena- 1905; Betty May – 1907; Charles Vincent Dean – 1909

Marguuerite

M.   Margo – 1937 M Edward Boardwell

Swen Alfredson B. Sweden

Twins:
    Debra   and
    Cynthia 1959

Debra M Butch Colby   Cynthia M. Alan Price

Greg   Christopher

Sarah   M..   Josh McGuire

William

Douglas – 1963 M. Christie   Douglas Il M. Jenny
                                David
                M. Tracey

Lorna   M Frank R. Adams   Audrey M . Emmett Beebee   Betty m Elmer Nichols

Charles Margrave (Nick) M. Lannie Beck

Penny -1935 M. Ron Munroe   Carl M Sherry
                        Chris M. Liz   Camille
                                    Megan
                        Jeff M. Karen   Abbey

Kelly M. Dr. Barton

    Tyler 1990

Lee M. Marci

Bradley   Kyle

Charles M. Dorothy Robarge (Nee O'Meara)

Judith Kathryn M. Harold Dean Brey   John Mack Ramsay M. Mary Hunt Wilson

Harold Dean, Jr. M. Debra Hiss   Jarl Joseph M. Amy Upjohn

    Elyse   Charlie

        M. Laura Hughson

        Mackenzie   Parker

CONTENTS

Morning Fare

HUEVOS RANCHEROS

I just loved Dinah Shore! She sang but I was not fond of her voice. She had a couple of TV shows, one of which I watched faithfully when I returned from a long day at the kid factory. She was so with it, dressed to the Tee, was athletic in that she played tennis and golf, dated the hunk, Burt (or was it Bert) Reynolds who was at least 20 years her junior, cooked up a storm and wrote a couple of cook books both of which I treasure.

Anyway, I found this recipe in one of her books and made it several times in the 1970s. My youngest son, Jarl, graduated from high school in 1980 and I took him to Cancun, Mexico before most people had heard of it. We stayed at a lovely hotel on the Caribbean where he tried Huevos Rancheros, and insisted that mine were better. Here is my version taken from the wonderful Dinah Shore.

2 Twenty-eight–oz. cans of tomatoes
2 Onions, finely chopped
¾ C. of Jack or Munster cheese
   and ¾ C. of sharp cheddar
   cheese mixed together
8 Jalapenos, (hot green chili
   Peppers) seeded

2 t. Oregano
Salt and pepper
4 Cloves garlic, finely chopped
2 Dashes Tabasco sauce
Olive oil
8 Poached eggs
4 Toasted tortillas

Saute onions and garlic in a little olive oil until translucent. Add tomatoes, oregano and Tabasco sauce. Add jalapenos and salt and pepper. Taste for seasonings. Simmer until sauce is reduced by one-half.

Poach 8 eggs. Toast tortillas by holding over a gas flame with tongs, or by sautéing on both sides in a little oil in a skillet. Drain on paper towel. Keep warm until ready to assemble.

Remove jalapenos from sauce with slotted spoon and set aside. On each tortilla, place 2 poached eggs, pour sauce over eggs and place 2 jalapenos on top.

Sprinkle cheese over top. Place under broiler just long enough to melt cheese.

Serves 4

EGGS MACK-MARGRAVE

My brother, Mack Margrave, was a professional musician, a 7th generation drummer. He made his home in Atlanta and ran and played with his myriad of friends on Sundays. They would have turtle races, kite flying contests and always food. This was one of his recipes that I have altered slightly.

I entered it into the Kalamazoo Gazette's Holiday contest one year and won a spot in the paper, but did not win the ultimate prize although the Chef judges took three paragraphs to praise this dish and vowed that it would be on their tables come Christmas morning.

4 English muffins (I prefer Bays) split and toasted
8 Large eggs, poached
1 Can of Campbell's garlic crème of mushroom soup
½ of above can of cream
½ C. of sour cream
Juice of ½ lemon
1 Scant t. powdered sugar
¼ Lb. fresh mushrooms
1 Small shallot, chopped finely
1 or 2 Jars of artichoke hearts
2 T. of sherry
Salt and pepper to taste
Sprinkles of paprika or chopped flat parsley for garnish

Sauté the mushrooms and scallion in olive oil until limp. Add mushroom soup, cream and sour cream, gently stirring with a whisk. Add lemon juice, heating just to a soft boil. Add the sherry just before serving.

Poach the eggs as you desire them and stack: toasted English muffin, artichoke hearts, poached egg followed by the sauce. Garnish with paprika or parsley.

Serves 4 quite generously

JIM HOLMBLADE'S OEUVES ET TARRAGON

Jim Holmblade was one of my best friends. He was probably 12 years older than I, loved to cook and so we would get in the kitchen and rattle around. He gave this lovely recipe to me one warm summer in the 1980s. Early in the 21st century he passed away and I miss him terribly.

Use ungreased custard cups   Oven at 350 degrees

Whipping cream, a small amount
Break an egg or 2 into it
Pour more whipping cream to cover eggs
Sprinkle a small amount of dry tarragon
Grate some fresh nutmeg on the top

Place the custard cup (s) in a pan of boiling water which you will set in the oven, take a look at them after 10-12 minutes. Remove when eggs have just set. This reminded me of an egg Julia might have poached. You may add salt and pepper after cooking.

BACON AND EGG CASSEROLE

1 Lb. bacon, cooked until crisp   2/3 C. half and half
2 C. Swiss cheese, shredded   1/3 C. shredded Parmesan cheese
8 Eggs

Line 13x9 inch pan with cooked bacon. Top with cheese, carefully. Without breaking yolks, place eggs on top of cheese evenly. Pour ½ and ½ over eggs and bake 8-10 minutes at 400 degrees. Sprinkle with Parmesan cheese and bake another 8-10 minutes.
Cut into squares around eggs.

SAUSAGE, EGGS AND HASH BROWNS

2 C. frozen hash brown potatoes
2 T. chopped onion
2 T. butter
1 C. shredded sharp Cheddar cheese
1 Lb. regular or hot sausage, cooked and drained

4 oz. sliced canned mushrooms
4 Eggs
½ C. milk
½ t. salt
¼ t. cracked pepper

Fry potatoes and onions in 2 T. butter until golden brown; place in greased 8 or 9- inch baking dish. Top with cheese. Crumble sausage and spread over cheese, top with drained mushrooms. Combine eggs, milk, salt and pepper; whip up well and pour over sausage. Bake at 350 for 30-35 minutes – serves 6.

ANOTHER BACON AND EGG CASSEROLE

1 dozen eggs
½ C. half-and-half
1 lb. bacon

8 oz. jar of mushrooms
4 oz. shredded cheddar cheese
2 cans cream of chicken soup
1 can mild

Scramble and fry 1 dozen eggs with ½ cup of half & half, dice and fry 1 lb. of bacon. Layer both in casserole dish (2 qt) along with 1 -8 oz. jar of mushrooms and 4 oz. shredded cheddar cheese, pour 2 cans of cream of chicken soup, diluted with 1 can of milk, over casserole. Bake at 350 degrees for 45 uncovered. Make ahead. Refrigerate and bake for 60 minutes, uncovered.

EGGS HUSSARDE – 1 SERVING

When Hal and Debra Brey, my eldest son and his wife, lived in New Orleans, I made a trip south to Louisiana to visit them one spring break. My dad had given me a cookbook, many years before, that had come from Brennans in the French Quarter, then known internationally for its French and Creole cuisine. I had really saved for the trip to the beautiful restaurant to treat my kids to an awesome brunch. Hal grumbled, screwed his face up and roared . . . ."No parking, narrow streets, crowded". . . and on infinitum. I was not to be talked down. Once we were seated in the garden and the first of the foods arrived, Hal began his Brey smile. We each ordered something different and ended with Banana's Foster which is also featured in this family food fare. Debra, as I remember, ordered Eggs Hussarde. I just heard yums and mmmmmmms so I found the recipe and am sharing with you her delight of the day.

2 Large thin slices ham, grilled   2 Slices tomato, grilled
2 Holland Rusks   2 Eggs soft poached
¼ C. Marchard de Vin sauce (recipe follows)   ¾ C. Hollandaise Sauce

Lay a large slice ham across each rusk and cover with Marchard de Vin Sauce. Cover next with tomato and then egg. Top with Hollandaise Sauce. Garnish with paprika.

Marchard de Vin Sauce:

¾ C. butter   2 T. minced garlic
1/3 C. finely chopped mushrooms   2 T. flour
½ C. minced ham   ½ t. salt
1/3 C. finely chopped shallots   1/8 t. pepper Dash cayenne
½ C. finely chopped onion   ½ C. red wine ¾ C. beef stock

In a 9-inch skillet melt butter and lightly sauté the mushrooms, ham, shallots, onion and garlic. When onion is golden brown, add flour salt, pepper and cayenne. Brown well, about 7 to 10 minutes. Blend in the stock and red wine and simmer over low heat for 35 – 45 minutes. Yields 2 cups

NANCY HISS GARDINER'S EGG CASSEROLE

Nancy is the twin sister of my daughter-in-law, Debra Brey. Like her identical siste, she is a giver. She is also artistic, great with color and design. She sews, quilts, is a great cook and gives hours and hours to her church. She made this one Sunday for me when I was visiting her home in Ann Arbor while her husband was working on his PhD in engineering.

1 Box croutons – garlic/onion   7 Eggs
1 Can mushrooms – small   ¾ C. half & half
1 Jar bacon pieces – 2 oz   8 oz. package shredded cheddar cheese

Beat eggs, add remaining ingredients and pour into a 9 x 13 greased pan. Put into a 350 degree oven for 30 – 35 minutes.
8-12 Servings

BACON AND CHEESE OMELET

12 Slices bacon   8 Eggs beaten
6 Slices pasteurized cheese   1 C. milk

Cook bacon, Drain and cool. Keep 1 slice for center of wheel. Chop 4 pieces and leave others whole. Cut cheese slices in half and place on bottom of lightly buttered pie pan. Beat eggs and milk together with fork. Add chopped bacon and pour over cheese slice. Bake in a preheated oven at 350 degrees for 30 minutes and arrange cooled bacon slices in a wheel on top and bake 10 minutes more. Let stand 5 minutes before cutting.

TERRI HANDLIN'S EGG CASSEROLE

Teri was a stunning young woman who babysat my boys, Hal and Jarl Brey, when they were tykes. She grew up to be a beauty, a long distance runner and worked in the same school district as I. She also served on the Board of Grand Rapids Community College, had a big voice in the feminist movement, and was married to Mike. I don't think that she enjoyed cooking because she used her oven as a storage place which made me chuckle. She did however have this recipe for me once and I quickly wrote it on a napkin where it still sits.

1½ Lbs. pork bulk sausage
18 Eggs
2 C. milk
1 ½ t. salt

3 C. shredded sharp cheddar cheese
3 C. garlic and onion flavored croutons
18 tomato slices

Heat oven to 325 degrees. While it's heating, cook sausage until light brown. Drain. Place sausage in greased baking dish. Beat eggs, milk and salt. Stir in cheese. Pour mixture over sausage. Sprinkle with croutons. Bake uncovered 45-50 min. Let sit 5 minutes before serving. Garnish with tomatoes, 18 servings.

BAKED FRENCH TOAST

8 Slices bread, cubed
1- 8 oz. cream cheese cut in small cubes
1 Dozen eggs

2 Cups milk
1/3 Cup syrup

Butter 9 x 13 pan, put in bread and cheese. Beat eggs, milk, & syrup, pour over bread. Refrigerate overnight. Bake 45 minutes at 350 degrees

BLUEBERRY FRENCH TOAST BAKE

1 Loaf French bread, cut in ½ inch cubes
1- 8 oz. package cream cheese cut in cubes
1 C. blueberries, fresh or frozen
12 Eggs beaten
1/3 C. honey or maple syrup

Sprinkle ½ of bread cubes in greased 9x13 in pan. Sprinkle the cheese cubes on the top, then the blueberries. Cover with remaining bread cubes. Mix the beaten eggs, milk and honey; pour over the top, pressing down to be sure all the bread is moist.

Refrigerate overnight. Remove from refrigerator 30 minutes before baking. Bake at 350 degrees for 30 minutes covered, then uncover and bake for 30 more minutes or until set. Serve warm, topped with Blue Berry Sauce which follows:

Blueberry Sauce

¾ C. sugar
2 T. corn starch
1 C. water

Simmer for 8-10 minutes until thick, and then add   .

1 C. blueberries
1 T. butter

Simmer until blueberries burst, then add butter.
Stir and serve warm over Blueberry French Toast Bake.

BLINTZES

I love these little things. One can find them in the frozen foods department and also find crepes ready-made in the same place—but I took a course one summer in the 1970's through Community Education to study the "crepe". The concept of crepes had just hit the USA; shops opened serving nothing but and everyone was making them at home. So here is my offering; it is nice if you have a crepe pan.

You can be creative as many people were and fill these babies with almost anything. I am, however, giving you my two favorites.

Makes 10

2 Eggs
2 T. salad oil
1 C. milk
¾ C. all-purpose flour

½ t. salt
Confectioners sugar
1 C. dairy sour cream

1) First make one of the fillings (see next page).

2) Make blintzes: In a medium bowl, beat eggs, salad oil and milk until well mixed. Add flour and salt and beat until smooth.
3) Refrigerate, covered 30 minutes. Batter should be consistency of heavy cream.

4) For each blintz: Melt ½ t. butter in a 10 inch skillet. Pour in 3 T. batter, rotate the pan quickly to spread batter evenly. Cook over medium heat until lightly browned on underside, then remove from pan. Stack blintzes, browned side up, as you take them from skillet.

5) Place about 3 T. of filling on the browned surface of each blintz. Fold two opposite sides over the filling: then overlap ends, covering filling completely.

6) Melt rest of butter in a large skillet. Add 3 or 4 blintzes, seam side down; sauté until golden brown on underside; turn and sauté other side. Keep blintzes warm in a low oven while cooking the rest.

7) Sprinkle with confectioners sugar. Serve hot with sour cream.
(see next page for fillings!)

Fillings for Blintzes—Choose one

Cheese filling
1 Pkg. (3 oz.) cream cheese
3 C. (1 lb.) ricotta cheese

1 Egg yolk
2 T. sugar
½ t. vanilla extract

In a medium bowl, combine cheeses, egg yolk, sugar and vanilla extract; beat until smooth. Refrigerate, covered until ready to use. Makes about 2 ½ cups.

Blueberry filling

1 Can (1 lb. 4 oz) blueberry pie filling
1/8 t. nutmeg

Combine pie filling and nutmeg in a small bowl. Mix well.

LIGHT AND FLUFFY PUMPKIN PANCAKES

2 C. reduced-fat biscuit mix
2 T. packed light brown sugar
2 t. ground cinnamon
1 t. ground allspice
1- 12 oz. can fat-free evaporated milk
1-2 C. solid pack pumpkin
1 T. vegetable oil
2 Eggs or ½ cup egg substitute
1 t. vanilla extract

In large mixer bowl, combine biscuit mix, brown sugar, cinnamon, and allspice. Add evaporated milk, pumpkin, oil, eggs, and vanilla; beat until smooth. Pour ¼ to ½ cup batter onto heated and lightly greased griddle. Cook until surface is bubbly. Turn. Cook until golden. Serve with warm maple syrup. Makes about 16 pancakes.

QUICHE

Betty Adams was a much older woman when I met her. Anything she touched in the kitchen turned into magic. I wish that I had her recipe file. . . .Everything was that good. She suffered from cancer and died quite soon after the diagnosis. This is her wonderful offering of quiche.

1-9 Inch unbaked pie crust, deep dish
1 Pkg. frozen broccoli
2 T. butter
½ Onion, sliced thin
12 Slices of bacon, fried and cut up. . .*or*
      under a ½ pound ham, cut up
1 C. (1/4 pound) grated Swiss cheese or cheddar

2 C. half and half
¾ t. salt
1 Pinch nutmeg

3 Eggs
1/8 t. pepper
1 Pinch cayenne pepper

1 package frozen chopped broccoli – use less . Saute onions in butter until soft. Sprinkle cut up ham or bacon onto crust. Spread onions and cover with cheese. Beat eggs, cream and spices until well mixed. Spread on crust. Put broccoli over top. Bake at 425° for 15 minutes, then reduce to 300 degrees for 40 minutes. This is sensational quiche.

MORNING ROLLS

Sue McLaughlin was one of my secretaries during my stint in education. I was very fond of her. She was great with kids, organized and ran a great home. This is her contribution.

24 Frozen uncooked dinner rolls
1- 3 ¾ Pkg. butterscotch pudding (not instant)
½ C. butter

¾ C. brown sugar
¾ t. cinnamon
½ C. chopped nuts

Arrange frozen rolls in a 9 x 13 pan. Sprinkle pudding over rolls. Cook butter and remaining ingredients until sugar dissolves (low heat) and mixture bubbles. Pour over rolls. Cover tightly with foil and let stand on counter top overnight. In the morning, bake at 350 degrees for 20 minutes. Let stand 5 minutes and invert on a good sized tray

CREAM CHEESE COFFEE CAKE
ALA DEBRA HISS BREY

All I have to do is ask my daughter-in-law, Debra, for a recipe and I get the best possible one that is to be found. This came from her mother, Peggy Hiss, and I absolutely can say that this is my favorite coffee cake in the whole wide world. So you enjoy!

(2) 8 oz. packages Pillsbury Crescent Rolls
(Room temp. for at least 30 min., but not more than 2 hours)
(2) 8 oz. packages Cream Cheese (Room Temp.)
1 Egg, separated
1 t. vanilla
1 C. sugar

Mix cream cheese, egg yolk, sugar and vanilla until light & fluffy. Stretch and spread 1 package crescent rolls onto 13 x 9 pan. Spread cream cheese mixture on top of crescent layer. Stretch and spread a second package of crescent rolls on top of cream cheese mixture. Beat egg white until frothy and brush on top layer of crescent rolls.

Topping:
1 t, cinnamon
½ C. sugar
½ C. chopped nuts

Mix together and sprinkle on top. Bake at 350 for 25-35 minutes.

\

SOUR CREAM COFFEE CAKE

2 Sticks butter
1 t. baking powder
1 ½ C. sugar
¼ t. salt
1 C. commercial sour cream
½ t. soda

2 Eggs, well beaten
1 C. finely chopped nuts
1 t. vanilla extract
1 ½ t. sugar
2 C. all-purpose flour
2 ½ t. ground cinnamon

Cream butter, sugar, and sour cream; add eggs and vanilla – beat well. Combine dry ingredients and add to creamed mixture; beat well. Thoroughly grease a 10-inch tube pan.

Make topping combing chopped nuts, sugar and cinnamon.

In bottom of the well-greased tube put a third of topping mixture, alternate layers of batter and topping ending with batter. Bake at 350 for 45 minutes.

MONKEY BREAD

3 Cans of Pillsbury Biscuits
1 C. white sugar
1 T. cinnamon
1 Stick butter
1 C. brown sugar

Mix together white sugar and cinnamon and place in a baggie Open the biscuits and cut in fourths. Put into the baggie with the mixture. Shake until well coated. Put in a large well greased pan. (Pam helps keep biscuits from sticking.) Melt butter in a saucepan. Add brown sugar to the melted butter. Boil one minute. Pour over biscuits. Bake in a 350 degree oven for 15 minutes. Check biscuits after they have baked for 25 to 30 minutes. Turn out of pan and break into pieces. They are good warm or cold. Makes a lot.

DEBRA BREY'S PUMPKIN BRAN MUFFINS

I just love my daughter-in-law. She is eldest son, Hal's wife of 30 years. Her name is Debra and she was raised on a farm, sews and quilts like a pro, and quietly goes about being a wonderful, giving human being. Sometimes she shares her Hiss family's recipes and I am always grateful.

1 ½ C. bran cereal – crushed
1 C. instant non-fat dry milk
3 Eggs
2 T. flour
2 T. sugar
1 t. baking powder
1 t. baking soda
1 ¼ t. cinnamon
¾ t. nutmeg
¼ t. clove
¼ t. ginger
1/-1/4 C. canned pumpkin

Combine dry ingredients, and then mix wet ingredients. Mix both together.
Spray tins with Pam and divide evenly into the cups. Bake at 350 degrees for 12 – 15 minutes (start watching at 12 minutes so muffins will be moist.
Let cool and freeze in pkgs. of 6.

STICKY ROLLS

Combine, heat slowly: 1 C. brown sugar
                            ½ C. butter
                            2 T. corn syrup

Spray Pam in tins, spoon the caramel mixture into muffin tins (20-24). Cut thawed, but cold bread dough with scissors into 8-10 pieces per loaf. Place each in a muffin cup, cover and let rise until almost doubled. Bake 375 degrees for 20 minutes. Cool 2 minutes. Invert.

PORK SAUSAGE BALLS IN PEACH HALVES

When I think about this dish, it makes me smile as it draws a lot of memories from college days. One of the meals fixed by a very snazzy young woman named Laurie Kolady, who is now gone, offered this dazzler. Everyone made fun of our eating this, but we did anyway and most of the time, we were so broke, that is all we had for dinner. Oh, the sacrifices one pays for an education! A great accompaniment to scrambled eggs.

1 #Lb. pork sausage
1 Egg beaten
2 T. minced onions
8 Canned peach halves

2 C. soft bread crumbs
24 Whole cloves
1/8 t. pepper & 1/4 t. salt
Peach syrup

Combine sausages, onion, bread crumbs, seasonings and egg. Form into 8 balls. Arrange peach halves. Stick 3 cloves around edge of each peach half; put sausage ball in center. Bake 45 minutes at 350. Drain off fat and pour on heated syrup, drained from peaches.

4 servings

COUSIN MARGO'S EGG AND CHEESE DISHES

Scramble 1 dozen eggs. Mix 1/2 cup milk, one 3 ounce can drained mushrooms, 1/2 cup grated cheddar cheese. Layer eggs and sauce in casserole and sprinkle top with bacon. Bake at 350 degrees for 1/2 hour.

Note: An option is to fry up one pound of bacon and crumble and put right in the egg mixture and mix all ingredients rather than layering. You can do this the night before and then just heat up in the oven prior to serving.

Jack Cheese Omelet   Combine 8 eggs and 4 green onions (thinly sliced) with 1/2 t. salt, 8 slices of bacon, 1 cup milk, and 2 1/2 cups shredded Monterey jack cheese. Cook bacon until crisp, drain and crumble. Saute onions in the bacon drippings. Drain and chop 1 can tomatoes, and beat egg, milk and salt. Put 2 cups cheese in 9 x 12 glass baking dish. Add bacon and onions and tomatoes. Pour over egg mixture. Bake 35-40 minutes at 340 degrees until set. Sprinkle with remaining cheese and return to oven until cheese melts. May be reheated or frozen and then reheated.

QUICHE LORRAINE

Quiches are favorites because they are an easy one-dish meal. The best Quiche Lorraine is great by itself, but with some imagination, quiche fillings are not limited to cheese.

Basic Quiche Lorraine with Cheese

1 C. unsifted flour
1/8 t. white pepper
1/3 C. margarine
1 t. salt
1/3 C. finely chopped onions
3 to 4 T. water

6 slices of crisply fried and bacon
1 T. margarine
Four eggs, beaten
¼ lb. Swiss cheese, diced
2 C. light cream
1/8 t. ground nutmeg.

Combine flour and ½ t. salt. Cut in 1/3 cup margarine until mixture resembles coarse meal. Gradually stir in ice water until mixture forms a ball. Roll dough out on lightly floured board to fit a 9-inch pie plate. Transfer to plate and shape edge. Saute onion in 1 Tbsp margarine until tender. Set aside to cool. Line prepared crust with crumbled bacon and diced cheese. Combine eggs, cream, remaining salt and spices and sautéed onion. Pour into crust and bake at 375 degrees for about 35 minutes or until knife inserted in center comes out clean. Serve hot.

Variations on the Basic Recipe

You can take the basic quiche recipe and fill with a variety of foods - 6-ounce can pitted olives drained, or one cup of chopped spinach seasoned with mustard and tarragon, one cup of sliced mushrooms and shallots, one cup cooked crab or lobster moistened with sherry – whatever you imagine would be good for this dish.

COUSIN MARGO'S
PULL APART CINNAMON ROLLS

These are so fabulous; they could be sold on a city corner in three minutes Margo's mother was Marguerite Margrave Alfredson, my father's sister. She was a cook of the best kind - - - everything she made was ever so good. She knew how to use spices and herbs, she knew how to bake up a storm and she passed all of her skills and recipes on to her daughter who gladly accepted them. She also could do any kind of handwork, was very intelligent yet meek. . . .And you know who inherits the earth! Margo inherited her mother's skills and remains one of the best cooks I know. Here is her recipe for sticky buns which she serves every Christmas to her waiting family.

1 pkg. frozen Rhodes rolls (16 small rolls)
2/3 cup chopped pecans
1 stick of butter & another ¾ stick

2 t. cinnamon
1 cup granulated sugar
1/3 cup brown sugar

1. Melt ¾ stick of butter, then add brown sugar – stir until melted
2. Grease a Bundt pan and pour above mixture in the pan
3. Sprinkle nuts on top of mixture above that is in the pan
4. Melt 1 stick of butter
5. In another bowl, mix granulated sugar and cinnamon
    Then
6. Dip each roll first in butter then granulated sugar and cinnamon – covering each roll
7. Arrange rolls in the Bundt pan
8. Pour remaining butter and then sugar and cinnamon mix over the rolls
9. Cover with tea towel and let set overnight
10. Bake at 375 for 30 minutes (the rolls raise overnight)

Let stand for 10 minutes or so after baking - Turn over on a plate and let stand for 5 minutes BEFORE removing the pan . . . . .serve warm

CHEESE STRATA

It says make it today, bake it tomorrow! Great for Christmas morning.

12 Slices white bread
8 oz. sharp cheese
1 Pkg. (10 oz) frozen chopped broccoli,
    cooked and drained
4 C. ham, cooked, diced
6 Eggs slightly beaten
3 ½ C, milk
3 T. onion, minced
¾ t. salt
¼ t. dry mustard
Dash of paprika
1 Can (10 ¾ oz.) condensed cream of mushroom soup, undiluted, heated

Cut circles from bread. Fit scraps of bread in 9 x 13 inch buttered pan. Over bread, layer cheese, broccoli, and ham in that order. Arrange bread circles over ham. Combine next 5 ingredients and pour over bread until it's saturated. Add a dash of paprika, cover and refrigerate overnight. Bake, uncovered at 350 degrees for 55 minutes. Let stand a few minutes before cutting. Top with heated, condensed mushroom soup.

Variations: Substitute 3 lbs. link sausage, browned and cut up for ham
             Substitute seafood (crab, shrimp, lobster) for ham
             Substitute 10 Oz. pkg, frozen spinach or asparagus for the broccoli

STRAWBERRY FRITTERS

2 Pts. fresh strawberries
1 C. buttermilk pancake mix
2/3 C. water

Powdered sugar
Whipped cream, optional

Wash whole strawberries and pat dry with paper toweling. Remove stem or leave intact. Mix pancake mix with water using rotary beater just until smooth. Dip berries in batter to coat all but stem. Fry in hot oil (400 degrees) until gold (about 30 seconds). Drain. Dust with powdered sugar. Offer whipped cream in desired for dipping. Serve at once.

BEIGNETS

Actually this is a French morning roll. Well, a pretty fancy one. These are served in threes along with a very strong demitasse of coffee in Jackson Square of The French Quarter in New Orleans. They are rather addictive and I have made them several times. These are also available in a box sold at The Olde World Market. But here is the from-scratch recipe.

¼ C. butter
1 ¼ C. water
1 ½ C. all purpose flour, sifted
3 Large eggs, beaten
½ t. vanilla extract
5 T. sugar

Incorporate all of the above ingredients and pat into a ball. Let sit in frig. for at least 30 minutes. Meantime heat fat in a deep skillet until it reaches 340 degrees. Roll out dough into a rectangle and cut it in squares. Carefully place the square dough into the fat and fry until golden brown. Remove and let drain on paper toweling. Sprinkle with confectioner's sugar and serve warm with coffee,

OVERNITE COFFEE CAKE

Another of my mother's gatherings!

Cream 2/3 C. butter and 1 C. brown sugar w/ ½ C. white sugar
Add 2 C. flour and 2 eggs
1 t. baking soda
1 t. baking powder
½ t. salt
1 C. sour cream

Pour ½ the batter in a 9x13 greased pan. Sprinkle 1 t. cinnamon mixed with ½ cup white sugar and sprinkle over batter. Pour other ½ of batter over and top with: ½ cup brown sugar, ½ t. nutmeg, ½ cup nuts.
Refrigerate overnight. Bake 350 for 35 minutes.

Notes

Breads

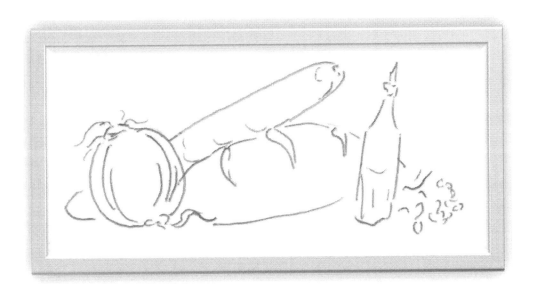

There is something wonderful about home made bread. I use a bread machine (now the 3ʳᵈ one I've had) because it's easy and will make a small loaf just for me or a larger one for when guests arrive or even a really large one for a gift. You can also make any of these by hand and stick them in the oven . . . . The aroma is heavenly!

IRISH SODA BREAD

I got into this bread after my visit to Ireland. It has a scrumptious old-country flavor. Makes a wonderful gift on St. Patrick's Day! I am giving you directions for a medium recipe in a bread machine.

½ C. old fashioned rolled oats (oat meal)
1¼ to 1 3/8 C. buttermilk
1½ T. butter
3 T. honey
1 t. salt
3 C. whole wheat flour
½ t. baking soda
1/3 C. golden raisins (optional)
3 t. Red Star Active Dry Yeast

Place all ingredients in bread pan, using the least amount of liquid listed in the recipe. Select Medium Crust setting then the whole wheat cycle and press start.

Observe the dough as it kneads. After 5 to 10 minutes, if it appears dry and stiff, or if your machine sounds as though it's straining to knead it, add more liquid 1 tablespoon at a time until dough forms a smooth, soft, pliable ball that is slightly tacky to touch.

After the baking cycle ends, remove bread from pan, place on cake rack, and allow to cool 1 hour before slicing.
(see next page for TLC additions)

TLC: Raw turnips cut into strips make a good snack or hors d'oeuvre.

TLC: Marinate fresh broccoli and cauliflower flowerets in Wishbone Italian Dressing.

TLC: Hot dog relish spread over a block of cream cheese is delicious served w/crackers

TLC: Top a large block of cream cheese with black or red caviar

WHOLE NUT BREAD

This recipe was given to my mother by a woman she worked with who was a fabulous cook. An old and secret recipe, it is by no means fruit cake (YUK!) I have made it every Christmas for 30 years.

4 eggs, separated	3 slices candied pineapple, cut up
1 C. sugar	1 Lb. whole pitted dates
4 T. wine	½ Lb. walnut halves
1 C. flour, sifted	½ Lb. whole candied cherries
1 t baking powder	½ Lb. pecan halves
½ t. salt	½ Lb. pound whole Brazil nuts

Beat egg yolks; add sugar, wine and cream all together.   Add fruit and nuts, then the flour, baking powder and salt alternately. With beaten egg whites, spoon into well greased pans lines with heavy brown paper; go ahead and use parchment paper in you wish and grease again (the paper) Bake at 350 degrees about an hour. Cool. Remove paper and store in refrigerator or freezer.

FRENCH BREAD

I'm not sure where I was when I met and started talking about bread making recipes with a lovely gentleman who quickly wrote down his recipe for this bread. It's quick and easy. By the way, his name was Bob Hubscher and I never ran into him again.

3 ¼ C. flour
1½ C. water
4 ½ t. sugar
½ t. salt
1 ½ - 2 T. dry yeast

Set on French or White and pusha da button!

POPOVERS

When I first discovered these (at a restaurant in East Lansing after and MSU game, having truly met O.J. Simpson when he played for Southern California University, was 19 years old (and hopefully then a good kid), I thought that I had died and gone to heaven. . . . .not because of the Simpson kid but for the popovers. And they are so very easy to make.

1 C. flour, sifted
½ t. salt

1 C. milk
1 T. salad oil   2 Eggs

Preheat oven to 425 degrees. Grease aluminum popover pans or large muffin tin (if you have an old iron popover pan, all the better). Pyrex custard cups may also be used, just grease them well and place on a baking sheet in the oven to heat thoroughly before filling. Measure all ingredients and place in a bowl and beat with a rotary beater until mixture is very smooth. It is a thin batter, so don't worry about that. Fill cups a little less than half full and bake in the preheated oven about 30 minutes WITHOUT PEEKING or until sides are rigid to the touch. If drier popovers are desired, pierce each one with a knife and bake five minutes longer.

BROTHER JUNIPER'S STRUAN BREAD RECIPE

I loved working the 10 years I spent at the Barnes and Noble book store. I coordinated all of the special orders and worked with a wonderful bunch of people. We considered ourselves one big dysfunctional family. I was madly searching through the cookbook section one week for a recipe called Struan bread—a healthy Scottish bread. Its secret ingredient is brown rice. One of the customers found it for me. I made it in my bread machine.

1 C. plus 2 T. water
2 ½ t. dry yeast- dissolved in the water
½ C. buttermilk
3 ½ C. flour
¼ C. polenta (cornmeal)   2 t. salt

¼ C. oats
2 T. honey
¼ C. wheat bran
¼ C. brown sugar
¼ C. freshly cooked brown rice

Put the ingredients in order into your bread machine and bake on white setting.
2 pound loaf.

HERB BREAD

Whenever I wanted sons Hal and Jarl to eat something, I told them it was German, so this was their German Herb Bread. They seemed to like it and they, of course, were Gourmands.

To 1/3 lb. sweet butter add 1 Tbs. finely chopped parsley, 1 heaping Tbs. finely chopped chives, ½ tsp. dried sweet basil and a few drops lemon juice.

Use a loaf of Italian or French bread cutting into thick slices almost but not quite through to the bottom, then cut through the middle the long way, being careful not to cut through the bottom.

Spread butter on cut sides, press back into loaf shape, wrap with foil and heat thoroughly in 350 degree oven.

BEER BREAD

My family really liked this as did anyone who received it as a gift. Warm it up a little and serve it with butter. Good old northern soul food and as easy as 1-2-3.

1 Can beer
2 T. sugar
3 C. self-rising flour

If you want to try a different twist, add
2 T. dried parsley flakes
1 ½ t. dill weed

Mix together, throw in a greased loaf pan and bake at 350 degrees for about an hour. When it comes hot from the oven, slather top with butter.

BUNDT CHEESE-ONION BUBBLE LOAF

This recipe was given to me many years ago by a favorite colleague, Carl Peterson, whose wife was an extraordinary Dutch cook.

2 loaves of frozen bread dough
1 C. shredded cheddar cheese
Combine – ½ C. melted butter and ½ envelope of dry onion soup mix

Cut each loaf into 12 slices. Poke indentation into each and fill with 1/24th of shredded cheese. Seal dough around cheese – to make a ball. Roll each ball in butter-onion mix. Then arrange in bundt pan. Let rise until doubled. Bake 30-35 minutes until golden brown. 350 degree oven.

COUSIN MARGO'S DATE AND CHEESE BREAD

¾ C. boiling water
1 Well beaten egg
½ Lb. dates, cut fine
¾ C. chopped nuts
1 C. grated cheese – use what you have on hand. . . .be creative

1¾ C. flour
1 t. salt
½ t. soda
½ C. sugar

Pour boiling water over dates and let stand for 10 minutes. Sift dry ingredients. Add dates, egg, cheese and nuts. Mix well and bake in a greased loaf pan at 350 degrees for 50 minutes

---

FOUR CRACKER RECIPES follow here.
I am always out of good crackers, so I went searching.

PECORINO CRACKERS – From Giada

1 ¼ C. grated pecorino Romano
½ t. salt
¼ t. freshly ground black pepper

1/8 t. cayenne
1 Stick unsalted butter, soften
1 C. all-purpose flour

Preheat oven to 350 degrees

Combine the cheese, salt, pepper, and cayenne in a medium bowl and stir to combine. Add the butter. Using a hand mixer, beat the cheese mixture and butter until combined. Add the flour, ¼ cup at a time, mixing only until incorporated and the mixture holds together. . . . Place Tablespoon-size balls of the dough on 1 to 2 parchment paper lined
baking sheets, tapping the dough down with your finger tips. Bake until just beginning to brown at edges, about 15 minutes. Let cool on baking sheet before transferring to a plate.

TLC: One most elegant "before" of all: lightly salted, lightly buttered, lightly toasted pecans.

CHEEZY COCKTAIL CRACKERS

1 C. butter, softened
1 lb. (2 cups) shredded sharp process cheese
2 C. sifted flour
½ t. salt
¼ t. cayenne pepper
¼ t. dry mustard
2 C. Total cereal

Place butter and cheese in large mixing bowl, mix thoroughly. Add flour, salt, pepper, mustard, mix well. Stir in cereal. Drop by rounded teaspoons onto greased baking sheet.

Flatten to ¼ inch thickness with fingers. Bake in slow over (325 degrees) about 18 minutes or until browned lightly. Note: crackers are good served warm. They also freeze well.

BLUE CHEESE AND WALNUT CRACKERS – from Ina

¼ Lb. (1 stick) unsalted butter at room temperature
8 Oz. Stilton cheese, crumbled (about 12 ounces with rind), at room temperature)
1 ½ C. all-purpose flour
2 t. kosher salt
1 t. freshly ground pepper
1 Extra-large egg beaten with 1 T. water for egg wash
½ C. roughly chopped walnuts

In the bowl of an electric mixer fitted with the paddle attachment, cream the butter and Stilton together for 1 minute, or until smooth. With the mixer on low speed, add the flour, salt and pepper and mix until it's in large crumbles, about 1 minute. Add 1 T. of water and mix until combined.

Dump the dough onto a floured board, press it into a ball, and roll into a 12-inch long log. Brush the log completely with the egg wash. Spread the walnuts in a square on a cutting board and roll the log back and forth in the walnuts, pressing lightly and distributing them evenly on the outside of the log.

Wrap in plastic and refrigerate for at least 30 minutes or for up to 4 days. You may freeze, but thaw completely before cutting.

Meanwhile preheat the oven to 350 degrees.
Cut the log 3/8ths thick with a small, sharp knife and place the crackers on a sheet pan lined with parchment paper. Bake for 22 minutes until very lightly browned. Rotate the pan once during baking. Cool and serve at room temperature.

PARMESAN AND THYME CRACKERS – One more from Ina

¼ Lb. (1 stick) unsalted butter
2 oz. grated Parmesan
1¼ C. all-purpose flour

1 t. chopped fresh thyme leaves
½ t. freshly ground black pepper
¼ t. kosher salt

Place the butter in the bowl of an electric mixer fitted with a paddle attachment and mix until creamy. Add the Parmesan, flour, salt, thyme and pepper and combine.

Dump the dough on a lightly floured board and roll into a 13-inch long log. Wrap the log in plastic wrap and place in the freezer for 30 minutes to harden.

Meanwhile preheat oven to 350 degrees.
Cut the log crosswise into ¼ to ½ inch thick slices. Place the slices on a sheet pan lined with parchment paper and bake 22 minutes.

COUSIN MARGO'S HERBAL BREAD

1 t. dry yeast
2¼ C. bread flour
1 t. salt
2 T. sugar
1 T. butter

2 T. chopped parsley
2 T. caraway seed
2 T. dill
7½ ounces water

Set your bread machine on 'White bread' – push start!

PISTACHIO BREAD

I think that one of my students gave me this in the '70s or '80s of the
20th century

1 Pkg. Duncan Hines Golden Butter Cake Mix
1 Pkg. Instant Pistachio Pudding
½ C. cooking oil
¼ C. sugar
¼ C. water
4 Eggs
Plus
½ pt. of sour cream

Combine and beat with mixer until smooth. Add ½ pint sour cream and mix
well. Pour equal amounts of batter into 2 greased and floured loaf pans reserving
1/3 of the batter.

Filling: 1 C. chopped walnuts or pecans
           1 T. packed brown sugar
           2 t. cinnamon

Sprinkle filling over and cover filling with remaining batter.
Bake 45 – 50 minutes in 375 degree oven. Cool, then remove from pans. May
glaze with 1 cup confectioners sugar and 2 Tb. milk.

SWEDISH LIMPA BREAD

I think that this and Scottish Struan bread are my favorites. My mother did not often bake or cook, but she could find the best recipes for a myriad of food. Like my sons, she probably was a gourmand, ever watchful for a winning fare. This came from one of her Swedish co-workers, a Ms. Johnson, and if you are from Sweden, you will pronounce it YON-SON!!

2 C. water
½ Cake yeast
½ C. brown sugar
2 t. caraway seeds
1 T. shortening

1 t. chopped orange peel or 1 scant tsp. anise seed
About 3 C. flour
1 t. salt
About 2 C. rye flour

Boil together water, caraway seeds, shortening and orange peel (or anise seed) for three minutes. Let mixture become lukewarm. Add yeast. Stir thoroughly, gradually add sufficient white flour to make a soft dough. Place dough in a warm place, cover and let rise for 1- 1 ½ hours. Add salt and enough rye flour to make a stiff dough. Let rise again for 2 hours. Knead slightly and shape into loaf. Put in to greased 9x5x3 (loaf pan) and let rise again for ½ hour. Bake in moderate oven at 350 degree oven for 1 hour. Makes 1 loaf.   God Bless my mama.

DEBRA BREY'S BRAN MUFFINS

If you are a WW, 1 muffin = 1 Point

1 ¼ C. bran
1 C. instant non-fat dry milk
¾ C. applesauce (no sugar added)
3 Eggs
3 T. raisins
2 T. flour

1 t. baking powder
1 t. baking soda
1 t. cinnamon
1½ t. honey
1/8 C. sugar

Mix dry ingredients. Add remaining ingredients. Bake in muffin pan sprayed with cooking spray at 350 degrees for 15 – 18 minutes.

ELAINE SELANDER'S MOTHER'S RYE BREAD

This recipe has to be 200 years old, Handed down from one Swedish woman to another, I am so blessed to have this in my little Irish hand. I loved Elaine Selander. She was so bright, a well of lore and a natural leader. She and my mother were good friends in their 20s, giving to their community, heading up Brownie Scouts, learning upholstery skills and anything to keep them busy. She recently passed away and I am glad that I connected with her before she left us.

4 C. rye flour
5-6 C. white flour
½ C. shortening
1 ½ T. salt
2 C. potato or warm water
1 C. sugar
2 C. scalded milk
½ C. molasses
3 cakes yeast (mixed with 1 T. sugar and ¼ C. warm water) set aside

Scald milk and add shortening and molasses. Cool to lukewarm. Mix rye flour, sugar and salt in large bowl. Add lukewarm liquids and yeast, mixing well with mixer after each addition. Add enough white flour to make dough firm to be kneaded (about 5 – 6 cups) Knead 'til elastic. Put in buttered bowl set in warm place. Cover and let rise till double. Cut dough in pieces and shape into loaves, punch with fork for air. Place in greased pans and let rise until double. Bake 350 degrees for about 45 – 50 minutes or until bread sounds hollow when tapped with fingers. Remove from pan and butter. Let cool on rack.

– MAKES 4 or 5 loaves

DEBRA BREY'S PUMPKIN BRAN MUFFINS

1¼ C. bran
1 C. instant non-fat dry milk
2 T. flour
2 T. sugar
1 t. baking powder
1 t. baking soda
1¼ t. cinnamon
¼ t. cloves
¾ t. nutmeg
Sprinkle of ginger
3 Eggs
¾ to 1 C. pumpkin
1½ t. honey
Mix dry ingredients; add eggs, pumpkin, honey - - stir some more
Bake 350 degrees 15 – 18 minutes

DEBRA'S APPLE AND BANANA OAT BRAN MUFFINS

4 oz. oat bran
4 Large eggs
4 t. vanilla
11/3 C. instant non-fat dry milk
4 t. baking powder
4 Pkg. Sweet and Low

2 or more t. cinnamon
1/8 t. nutmeg
Pinch of cloves
1 Small banana, mashed
2 Small shredded apples (w/peelings)
¼ C. water

Mix dry ingredients, then mix wet ingredients. Add both together. Spray tins really well with Pam and divide evenly into 24 cups. Makes 24 muffins.

Bake at 350 degrees for 12 to 15 minutes (start watching at 12 minutes so muffins will be moist). Let cool and freeze in pkgs. of 6

DATE AND NUT LOAF

1 C. chopped dates
1 Egg
1 C. boiling water
1 C. walnuts, coarsely chopped
1 T. butter

1 t. soda
1½ C. flour
1 C. sugar
1 t. vanilla

Sprinkle dates with soda and pour boiling water over all. Set aside. Cream the sugar, butter, and egg. Gradually stir in walnuts, flour, and vanilla. Combine with date mixture.

Pour into ungreased, paper-lined loaf pan. Bake at 350 degrees for 40 to 45 minutes.

Makes 1 loaf

ICE BOX ROLLS

1 C. shortening
2 Eggs, beaten
1 C. sugar
2 Cakes of compressed yeast

1½ t. salt
1 C. cold water
1 C. boiling water
6 C. unsifted flour

Pour boiling water over shortening. Add sugar and salt. Let cool until tepid. Dissolve yeast in a little of other cup (cold water) for 5 minutes and stir. Then add to other ingredients. Add beaten eggs. Beat in flour. Put into refrigerator 4 hours before ready to use. About 3 hours before wanting to use, roll into desired shapes, using just enough extra flour to make easy to handle. Put in greased pans and allow to rise at room temperature for an hour or more, until double original size. Bake in 425 degree oven for 12 – 15 minutes. If harder crust is desired, bake in 350 – 375 oven for 20 minutes.

TLC: Serve fresh strawberries in orange juice at breakfast.

AUNT LORNA'S CHEESE BREAD

Mix: 2 T. dry yeasts   ½ C. warm water
      1 t. sugar

1 C. scalded milk   1 C. sugar
5 C. flour   2 C. sharp grated cheese
1 t. salt

Stir sugar and salt into hot milk. Cool. Add yeast mixture and mix thoroughly. Beat half of flour into mix until dough is smooth. Add grated cheese and enough of remaining flour to make a stiff dough. Knead on board 8-10 minutes. Put in greased bowl, cover with damp towel and let rise in warm place until double. Punch down. Shape into two loaves and put into greased bread pans. Let rise until double

Bake 35 minutes in 375 degree oven

SUE D'S LEMON BREAD

2 Sticks butter softened   5 Large eggs
2 C. sugar   3 T. finely grated lemon peel from 4 large lemons
1 t. baking powder   ¾ C. buttermilk
½ t. baking soda   ¼ C. lemon juice
½ t. salt   3 C. flour

Beat butter, sugar, baking powder, soda and salt on medium for 3 minutes. Add 1 egg at a time. Add lemon peel. Combine buttermilk and lemon juice. Alternate with flour to butter mixture.

Pour into 5 mini-loaf pans. Smooth top of batter. Bake 350 for 30-35 minutes. Let pans cool on rack for 10 minutes. Remove from pans. Poke holes in loaves with toothpick. Brush with lemon syrup.

Lemon syrup: ¼ C. sugar
                ¼ C. + 2 T. lemon juice

Boil until sugar dissolves. Totally cool.
Whisk 1 C. confectioners sugar with 2 T. lemon juice. Frost loaves.
Sprinkle with ¼ cup chopped pecans.

JULIE CRYSTAL PETRIE'S ZUCCHINI BREAD

I met Julie as a colleague when she was in her 20's. She had just finished her graduate work and joined our staff in the counseling center of Forest Hills Central High School. Time simply flies when you're having fun! She retired last year (same school, same office) and was able to put all of her creative efforts into her house on the Thornapple River. She gave me this recipe many years ago and I have kept it safe.

Mix:
3 Eggs
2 C. sugar
1 C. vegetable oil

2 C. zucchini, chopped
3 t. vanilla

Mix:
3 C. flour
1 t. salt
1 t. soda

¼ t. baking powder
3 t. cinnamon
1 C. chopped walnuts

Mix both together. – Heat oven to 350°. Bake in 2 loaf pans that have been well greased for 50 or 60 minutes.

TLC: Wrap chunks of melon with very thin slices of prosuitto ham.

TLC: Remember: Line silver dishes with glass bowls, doilies, Saran wrap, aluminum foil etc. against salt, vinegar, mayonnaise and other evil silver spoilers and pitters.

TLC: For an easy transition to dinner, serve a first "course" in living room. Soup in mugs, an antipasto plate or an elegant plate of shrimp.

TLC: Thin slices of baked chicken breasts, watercress and mayonnaise (with chutney and curry powder added) on whole grain bread.

TLC: Keeping bread in the freezer prevents moldy throw-aways. Bread frozen fresh will thaw to original softness in minutes.

SOUTHERN CORN BREAD OR CORN STICKS

Mac MaGill was another favorite person of mine. He lived with his wife, Lucille, around the corner in East Grand Rapids and adored our dog, Ralph Bunch. Mac was southern from his head to his toes and still talked about the Yankees and The War. I have a treasured and precious quilt his grandmother made by hand…and this recipe which was his mother's. In addition, he gave me the very heavy corn stick pan for baking this bread. I lost both Mac and Lucille as well as Ralph Bunch around the same time. So I treasure the recipes as a remembrance (Lucille's may be found in other places within the book).

1 Egg
1 Pt. of thick buttermilk
1 Pt. white cornmeal
1 t. salt
1 t. soda
1 t. baking powder
Add: 1 t. sugar and 1 T. shortening

Notes

Soups

JULIE RISKO NEELY'S
BUTTERNUT SQUASH SOUP

Julie Risko was from the class of 1988 at Forest Hills Northern High School. She was its president, a cheerleader, an early college enrollment student at Kendall College of Art and Design and later accepted at The Rhode Island School of Art and Design, one of the country's premiere art schools. She worked her way through college and did well academically, later joining an artistic art firm in Chicago which ultimately named her creative art director. I am very proud of this kid who last year turned 40 along with the rest of that magic class. She is a creative cook as well as the mother of two very active boys, Calder and Spencer and married to Kenn. A favorite person of mine, we still keep in contact and get together when I train it to The Windy City.

4 T. unsalted butter
1 Large shallot, finely chopped
3 lb. butternut squash
   Cut in ½ lengthwise and each ½
   Cut in ½ widthwise (save seeds and strings)
6 C. water
Salt
½ C. heavy cream
1 T. dark brown sugar
Pinch of freshly grated nutmeg

Melt butter in stock pot. Add shallots and sauté until translucent then add seeds and strings. Stir over low heat until a pretty saffron color. Add water and salt bringing to a boil. Turn heat to medium low. Add squash, cut side down in steamer basket to pot. Cover four about 30 minutes. Set squash aside and strain steaming liquid. Dump the seeds and strings. Scrape out squash when cool. Puree squash in blender until smooth. Transfer to clean pot and add remaining liquid, cream, brown sugar, and nutmeg. Salt to taste.

TLC: A dash of nutmeg adds a great taste to cream soups.

TLC: Use a wire whisk for smooth blending of canned soups and water.

COUSIN MARGO'S PLETHORA OF SOUP CONCOCTIONS

Remember, anything she makes is terrific. Enjoy!

Ground Beef Soup

1 C. chopped onions
1 Lb. ground beef
1 C. raw cubed potatoes
½ C. diced celery
1 #2 Can or 2 ½ cups tomatoes
1 C. diced raw carrots
1 C. shredded cabbage
1 Qt. water

½ t. thyme
1/8 t. pepper
¼ t. basil
2 t. salt
1 Small bay leaf
¼ C. uncooked rice

Brown meat and onion in pan – drain fat. Add potatoes, celery, tomatoes, basil and salt. Bring to a boil (more tomatoes may be added if desired). Sprinkle in rice. Add bay leaf, carrots, cabbage, thyme, pepper and water. Cover and simmer one hour or until it is done. Remove bay leaf. Makes a large kettle.

All Day Pea Soup

2 Pkg. (32 oz.) split green peas and 7 cups water
1 ½ Lb. of pork hocks or a nice ham bone
2 C. diced potatoes
1 ½ C. chopped onions

1 C. cubed celery
1 C. sliced carrots, and a little salt

Rinse peas under cold running water and drain. In large bowl combine all ingredients and put in the refrigerator overnight. Cover bowl. Place in slow cooker on low for 6 – hours. Before serving remove meat and cut into bite size pieces and return to soup. You may want to add more water if the soup is thicker than you like.

Diet Soup

A great tasting soup that does not contain many calories:

1 head of shredded cabbage, 1 qt. stewed tomatoes, 3 stalks chopped celery, 1 diced onion and 1 can mushrooms (drained) 1 can green beans. Put on stove or slow cooker for several hours. Store in refrigerator . . . heat and eat as you wish.

Another Version Called TJ Soup

Shred in processor: 1 Onion
                            1 Head cabbage
                            1 Stalk celery
2 Large cans tomatoes - - - - - puree in processor
1 Pkg. Knorr's French Onion Soup
4 C. water

Put all in crock pot or Dutch oven. Bring to boil for 20 minutes. Turn down and simmer for 2 hours. Supposedly you can eat all you want because it is soooooooo good for you!

Hearty Soup Mix

A tasty nutritious time-saver to use with your favorite soup stock. Also a great gift at holiday season when packed in a jar with a bow and directions for use. They will appreciate a quick way to provide a whole meal in a brief time.

12-oz. package any type small macaroni
12-oz. package dry green split peas
11-oz. package pearl barley
16-oz. package lentils
2 C. long grain rice
¼ C. dried parsley flakes

3 T. oregano leaves
2 Jars (1.5 oz. each) dried, minced
                         onion

Combine ingredients and put in airtight container. Yield: 16 cups (1 gallon dry soup mix). Label and store in cool, dry place.

To use Hearty Soup Mix: Use any meat (ham hocks, soup bone, stew beef, or hamburger), 2 bouillon cubes, and cook until tender in enough water to yield 5 cups. Add 1 cup soup mix and cook 30 minutes. Add fresh vegetables of your choice, such as 2 carrots, 1 ½ cups cabbage, and 3 stalks celery. Yield: 6 – 8 servings

Asparagus Soup

4 – 6 C. of asparagus
6 C. milk
1 ½ C. water
4 T. water
Cheese

2 T. cornstarch
3 Chicken bouillon cubes
½ C. finely chopped onions
½ Large brick Velveeta

Cut up asparagus in ½ inch pieces. Add ½ cup finely diced onion. Put this is a cooking pot. Ad 3 chicken bouillon cubes and 1 ½ cups water. Cover pot with lid and cook on medium until asparagus is tender (about 5-7 minutes). Pour in milk and dice up ½ of a large block of Velveeta cheese and stir into soup until cheese is melted. Mix 2 tablespoons of cornstarch into 4 T. of water and stir into hot soup. Stir until thick. You can add more cornstarch and water if soup is not as thick as you want.

Variety Soups

One of the easiest ways to create soup is to combine cans of condensed soup you have already purchased. One of the popular soup companies came up with over 400 combinations - - we have listed a few or our own for you to try, including using canned meat and vegetables.

Clam Chowder and Corn

Use one can of clam chowder and one can of creamed corn. Mix in a pan with one cup of milk.

Broccoli Chicken Soup

Use one can creamy chicken mushroom soup. Put in pan and then add a 10 oz. package of frozen broccoli. Cover and simmer until broccoli is tender.

Soup of Navy Wives

In the 1960's, Cousin Margo's husband, Ed was serving his country in the Navy. Short of money, some of their get togethers with other Navy couples called for each couple to bring one item to put in a big pot to create their meal. One can of corned beef (crumbled), or leftover chicken, or cooked ground beef – or just use canned vegetables – season to taste. Every couple added what ever vegetable they brought, i.e. peas, corn, green beans, tomatoes, kidney beans etc. All ingredients were heated in a large pot and they never found a soup concoction that they did not like. Be creative – try a soup of Navy wives - -use your imagination to creative your own meal. I say Amen to that!

BRAVO MUSHROOM SOUP

I belonged to a book club at the beginning of the 21st century. We collected about twelve women of all ages, read a designated book, and discussed it. One of the women was a marvelous cook. No matter what she made, it was glorious. Her name was Evie Vroegop and I still can't pronounce her last name. This is one of the soups she served to us all one stormy night and she was kind enough to share the recipe with me.

1 oz. olive oil
1 Stalk celery, diced small
1 Small carrot, diced small
1 Lb. mushrooms, slices
2 t. garlic, minced
4 oz. white wine

1 ½ C. chicken stock
1 Pt. heavy whipping cream
4 oz. tomato juice
3 T. cornstarch (dissolved in ¼ cup water)
1 C. Parmesan cheese, freshly grated
Salt and pepper to taste

In a large pot over high heat add the oil, celery, and carrot. Cook until soft, approximately 5 minutes. Add the mushrooms and continue to cook, stirring often, until soft. Approximately 10 minutes. Stir in garlic and cook for 3 minutes. Add wine and simmer for ten minutes. Add chicken stock, whipping cream, and tomato juice. Stir in corn starch to thicken and simmer 5 minutes, stirring constantly to avoid burning. Remove from heat and stir in cheese, salt and pepper.

EVIE VROEGOP'S CHICKEN SOUP

1 Whole chicken
Minor's soup base
6 C. water
1 C. long grain rice (the long cooking kind or
                    2 cups Egg noodles)
1 C. celery, chopped (throw in some leaves)
1 C. carrots, chopped thin
1 C. onions, diced
1 Can cream of chicken soup
2 Cups cold water
Salt and pepper to taste
Some shavings of nutmegs, to taste

Cook the whole chicken. Debone and save broth. Start with chicken pieces, the broth, and Minor's soup base – about 1 – 2 T. and 6 C. of water. Add long grain rice and bring to a boil. Add celery, carrots, onions and simmer for 30 minutes. Add 1 can of cream of chicken soup and 2 cups cold water. Whisk this into soup mixture. Add salt, pepper and nutmeg to taste. If you prefer noodles, add them near the end of cooking time, say when the veggies have cooked 25 minutes so noodles will not become mushy.

WHITE CHICKEN CHILI
FROM THE FRIER FAMILY

Dino is the cook in the Frier family. He was born in Greece and brings a plethora of ethnic recipes each night when he cooks. His wife, Mollie is a friend of mine and knows that she is fortunate not to perform chef wizardry each night. She decorates their beautiful home and paints. Anyway this is their combined recipe and I have enjoyed it often enough to ask for it.

The amounts you use depend on how many you are cooking for. . . .you can freeze this very nicely also.

Cooked diced chicken
Large jar of Great Northern White Beans, undrained
Large jar of salsa, degree of heat depends on your taste
Large can of chicken broth
1 to 2 t. cumin
Pepper Jack cheese –shredded Monterey Jack w/jalapeno peppers

Mix together in order in a large soup pot, add shredded cheese last and stir until it has melted. Serve with corn muffins.

CHILI

I found this recipe in a one of the mystery books I was reading. The peanuts were an added surprise.

½ C. peanut oil
2 C. onions, chopped
5-6 Cloves garlic, minced
2 lbs. ground beef
1-15 oz. can stewed tomatoes
½ C. strong black coffee
2/3 C. whole peanuts

2/3 C. chopped roasted peanuts*
½ Small can tomato paste
2 – 4 T. chili powder
1 T. salt
1 t. oregano
1 t. cumin

(continued on next page)

Use a very large pot to sauté onions and garlic. Add the ground beef when the onions and garlic have wilted in the peanut oil. After browning, add the tomatoes, coffee, chopped peanuts, tomato paste and spices. Cover or put in a crock pot to simmer for a few hours. Just before serving, add the whole peanuts to the top of chili which you have placed in a strong soup tureen.

Corn muffins, Mexican spoon bread or Johnny cake might be nice to serve with this. *Be sure to tell any guests that this has peanuts in it because of allergies.

CHILI CON CARNE

There was a lovely woman who lived a few doors down the beach from Cousin Penny, Aunt Lorna and Uncle Frank by the name of Mrs. Spicklemire who loved Penny dearly. I have to add a recipe from her in honor of that friendship. So enjoy her Chili Con Carne. With crackers, a green salad and light dessert, this is a good, filling meal

In Cubes: 2 lbs. lamb shoulder
1 lbs. pork shoulder

1 Can red kidney beans
1 Cup chopped pitted ripe olives (optional)
1 Medium onion, minced

Sauce:

1 Minced onion
2 Cloves garlic - - minced
1 T. hot oil
1 T. chili powder
1 t. salt

½ t. thyme
1 Bay leaf
2 C. meat stock
1 C. tomato puree

Make sauce by browning in hot oil the onions and garlic. Add spices, meat stock and tomatoes.

Cut lamb and pork in small cubes and brown in fat with onions and garlic. Add spices, meat stock and tomatoes. Add sauce and simmer 2 hours. Add kidney beans and olives.

CHICKEN SOUP FROM MY BEST OREGON GAL PAL, FLORENCE OBSTFELDT

1 Chicken
Peppercorns
1 Bay leaf
Cloves
Thyme

Parsley
Celery
Onion
Carrots
Water to cover

Within first hour of cooking chicken – you must skim off the scum and wipe down inside of pot to get hiding scum. Cover partially. Strain through cheese cloth and refrigerate. (Then make chicken salad with meat). Can add chicken bullion if not rich enough.

WHITE CHICKEN CHILI

Oscar Solis of Mexican decent and with whom I worked at Barnes and Noble gave me this recipe. His mother was an amazing cook, sending many and wonderful Mexican dishes to work with Oscar which we all devoured.

4 Boneless chicken breasts, cut into ½ inch cubes
1 White onion, chopped
2 Cloves garlic, minced
2 Stalks celery, chopped
3 Jalapeno peppers, seeded and sliced
1 – 10 oz. pkg. white shoe peg corn

1-15 oz. can chicken broth
1 t. ground cumin
2 t. chili powder
½ t. red pepper
1- 16 oz can navy beans

This is so easy! Throw all ingredients in a crock pot on low and let go all day. The aroma is divine! When serving add chopped parsley and shredded cheese for garnish.

MATTIE BERMAN'S LENTIL SOUP

One summer day, I visited Edna Blomdahl, one of Whitehall's First Ladies and a lifelong friend of my mother's. She and her husband. Leonard (a very favorite person of mine) owned the local grocery. Edna wrote a weekly food column for The Whitehall Forum, our small town newspaper, collected antiques, hooked rugs and cooked wonderful dishes. Her husband, Leonard had the most beautiful yard in town, working all spring, summer and fall to make it so. He restored antiques in the winter. Whenever I came back home to visit, I would stop to see this interesting couple. Leonard, without fail, made up a magnificent bouquet of his gardens' flowers for me. These two are now gone and I miss my visits and their eager faces when guests would arrive. When I stopped this particular summer, Edna and I got to talking about people who were no longer with us and how recipes truly leave an indelible mark for future people to remember them. This recipe is one of Mattie Berman's, wife of the editor of the local newspaper and mother to a couple of school friends of mine. Do enjoy as much as I have! This soup was also served at my 50th birthday party.

2 C. lentils 1 #
2 C. onions sliced
1 C. carrots, sliced
6 t. salt
1 beef soup bone

1 C. celery, sliced
1 Clove garlic, finely chopped
11 C. cold water
1 C. canned or fresh tomatoes

Simmer all - save tomatoes - for 1 ½ hours – add tomatoes and simmer another hour or until lentils are done. Mattie always purchased short ribs – using this meat in the soup. Serve with a slice of lemon.

FRENCH ONION SOUP

1 Can Campbell's French onion soup
Season with your favorite spices, Worcestershire etc.
1 Can Campbell's consumé
1 C. good dry red wine

Simmer together for 1 hour. Place in soup crocks with parmesan cheese, 1 round Dutch rusk and 1 round of provolone cheese. Place in oven either under broiler or until cheese is melted in slow oven.

QUICK VERSION OF FRENCH ONION SOUP

Heat oven to 400°

3 14-oz. cans ready-to-eat beef broth
¾ C. canned French-fried onions
1/3 C. dry sherry

4 Slices stale French bread
4- 1-oz. slices Swiss cheese

Arrange four 10-oz. oven-safe soup bowls on a baking sheet. Divide broth and onion among them. Add 1 T. of sherry to each. Float bread, top w/cheese. Bake 12-15 min.

MINESTRONI

Eldest granddaughter, Elyse and grandson Charlie have another grandmother named Betty Upjohn who in her own right is a great and learned cook. She broke bread one evening with: yes, you guessed it, Julia and Paul Child. Can you just imagine having dinner with Julia? Betty insisted that she was like an old shoe so I'm sure that I would have been comfortable just listening to one of the great ladies of cookery talk about anything. Betty was kind enough to share with her community via The Junior League Cookbook, a recipe for minestrone which I made for my infamous soup party on my 50th birthday. It is divine!

¼ Lb. lean salt pork, diced
1 Qt. rich beef stock
1 C. potatoes, cut in large cubes
1 C. carrots, cut in large pieces
1 C. turnips, cut in large pieces
¾ C. rice, uncooked
1 C. onions, sliced
½ C. green peas
½ C. lima beans
¼ Small head of cabbage, shredded
4 Medium tomatoes, diced or 3 cups canned
Parmesan cheese, grated (for garnish)

¼ Lb. fresh spinach, shredded
1 Leek (white part only), shredded
½ C celery, sliced in large pieces
2 T. tomato paste
2 T. parsley, chopped
½ t. sage
½ t. ground black pepper
Salt to taste

Cook pork in water to cover in a large covered kettle for 30 minutes. Add stock, bring to a boil. Add potatoes, carrots, turnips, and rice. Cover and cook for 10 minutes, add all remaining ingredients except Parmesan cheese. This is very thick and vegetables are tender.

Serve as a main dish, sprinkled with Parmesan cheese. Note: soup may be thinned with chicken broth.

Yield: 12 8-oz servings

FRESH TOMATO SOUP

3 Slices bacon, chopped
1 C. chopped onion (1 large onion)
½ C. chopped celery (1 stalk)
2 ½ Lb. tomatoes, peeled and quartered (if you wish to seed them, do)
1 C. water
2 T. sugar
1 t. salt
1 T. pickling spices
¼ C. snipped fresh parsley
½ t. lemon juice
 Lemon slices, halved (optional)

In a large saucepan, cook bacon until crisp. Remove bacon from pan with a slotted spoon, reserving drippings in pan. Drain bacon on paper towels; set bacon aside. Stir onion and celery into drippings. Cook over medium heat about 5 minutes or until vegetables are tender, stirring occasionally. Add tomatoes, water, sugar and salt. To make a spice bag, cut a double thickness of 100-percent-cotton cheesecloth into an 8-inch square. Place pickling spice in center. Bring up corners; tie with cotton string. Add to saucepan. Bring to boiling reduce heat. Cover and simmer for 20minutes. Remove and discard spice bag. Let mixture cool slightly.

Place half of the tomato mixture in a blender container or food processor bowl. Cover and blend or process until almost smooth; pour into a large bowl. Repeat with the remaining mixture. Return all to the saucepan. Stir in parsley and lemon juice; heat through.

Ladle into bowls and, if desired, garnish with lemon slice. Top each serving with crisp-cooked bacon. Makes 5 side-dish servings (160 calories each!!!) This can be frozen.

TLC: Homemade biscuits can be undercooked to be "brown 'n serve". To heat: Brush with butter and put in hot oven for 5 minutes.

TLC: Keeping bread in the freezer prevents moldy throw-aways. Bread frozen fresh will thaw to original softness in minutes.

SWEET POTATO SOUP WITH BUTTERED PECANS

¾ C. finely chopped onion
1 C. finely chopped leeks, washed well and drained
2 Large garlic cloves, minced
3 Large carrots, sliced thin – about 1 ½ cups
1 Bay leaf
3 T. unsalted butter
2 Lb. (about 3 large) sweet potatoes
½ Lb. russet (baking) potatoes
5 C. chicken broth plus addition for thinning the soup if desired
¾ C. dry white wine
1½ C. water

For buttered pecans: ¾ C. chopped pecans
                        2 T. unsalted butter
Crème fraiche or sour cream as an accompaniment

Make the soup: In a kettle cook the onion, the leek, the garlic, and the carrots with the bay leaf and salt and pepper to taste in butter over moderate heat, stirring, until the vegetables are softened. Add the sweet potatoes, peeled, halved lengthwise, and slice thin, the 5 cups broth, the wine and the water, simmer the mixture, covered for 15 to 20 minutes or until the potatoes are very tender, and discard the bay leaf. In a blender puree the mixture in batches until it is very smooth, transferring it as it is pureed to a large saucepan, add the additional broth to thin the soup to the desired consistency, and season the soup with salt and pepper. The soup may be made 1 day in advance, kept covered and chilled, and reheated.

Make the buttered pecans:
In a skillet cook the pecans in the butter with salt to taste over moderate heat, stirring occasionally, for 10 minutes, or until they are golden brown, and transfer them to paper towels to drain. The pecans may be made 2 days in advance and kept in an airtight container or resealable plastic bag.

Divide the soup among bowls and top each serving with a dollop of the crème fraiche and some of the buttered pecans. Makes about 11 cups, serving 8 to 10

GAZPACHO

So healthy! Found this one years ago and try to make it once a year during the summer when everything is fresh.

¼ C. almonds, ground
2 Shallots, peeled and chopped
1 t. salt
1 t. white pepper
1 C. extra virgin olive oil
½ C. cider vinegar
2 Eggs
2 Medium cucumbers peeled, seeded, chopped

1 t. ground cloves
1 t. ground cumin
Cayenne pepper to taste
3 Slices stale white bread, crusts removed
4 C. chicken stock
1 C. whipping cream, unwhipped
1 Can (16 oz.) Italian tomatoes

Put almonds, shallots, salt and white pepper in a food processor and blend until smooth. Set aside in a bowl. Blend remaining ingredients until everything is mixed but not smooth. Pulsate the processor. Add to first mixture. Chill.

ANOTHER LESS COMPLICATED VERSION OF GAZPACHO

1 Clove garlic, crushed
6 T. lemon juice
3 C. fresh tomatoes, peeled and chopped
½ C. chopped green pepper
½ C. chopped shallots
¼ C. flat leaf parsley, chopped
2 C. peeled, chopped cucumber
2-3 t. Salt (test before adding the 3rd t.)
Tabasco sauce to taste
1/3 C. extra virgin olive oil
2 C. tomato juice

Mix together all ingredients in a food processor and chop, chop, chop until mixed. Chill.

LOBSTER–SHRIMP CHOWDER– Very Easy

When I turned 50, I threw myself a surprise party. I invited 70 and 50 showed up waiting for 6 different kinds of soup and home baked bread. Here is one that was the biggest hit.

¼ C celery, finely chopped   *Louis Kemp makes a good imitation
2 T. shallots, finely chopped   for either of these – just chop them up
2 T. butter
1 Can (10 ¾ oz) condensed Cream of shrimp soup
1 C. (10 ¾ oz) condensed Cream of Mushroom soup
1 Soup can milk
1 C. half-and-half
1 Can (5 oz) lobster or crab meat (or equivalent frozen*)
¼ C. dry sherry
1 T. flat leaf parsley, chopped

Cook celery and shallots in butter until until tender. Add shrimp and mushroom soups, milk and half-and-half. Heat through.

Add lobster, sherry and parsley just before serving. Heat through.

KING'S ARMS TAVERN
CREAM OF PEANUT SOUP

Brought back from Williamsburg, VA by a friend of mine – serves 10-12

1 Medium onion, chopped
2 Ribs celery, chopped
¼ C. butter
3 T. all-purpose flour
Peanuts, chopped
2 Qts. chicken stock or canned chicken broth
2 C. smooth peanut butter
1 ¾ C. light cream

Saute onion and celery in butter until soft, but not brown. Stir in flour until well blended. Add chicken stock, stirring constantly, and bring to a boil. Remove from heat and puree in food processor or blender. Add peanut butter and cream, stirring to blend thoroughly. Remove to low heat, but do not boil, and serve garnished with chopped peanuts.

Note: This soup is good served ice cold as well.

Salads

BETH HUEBNER'S CURRIED RICE SALAD

Beth was one of my favorite students from the class of 1974. She was bright, world aware and giving. She moved to the west coast and lived in the rural-ness of Albany, Oregon where I visited her one beautiful summer. She had married George and proudly introduced me to her three lovely children of whom she was an extraordinary mother. I miss her love of life and interest in the world and its culture. She gave me this recipe which I have cherished. I make it a couple of times a year to take to gatherings since it renders a pretty big salad.

4 C. cooked chilled rice
4 green onions, chopped
3 stalks celery, chopped
1 can pitted black olives

½ C. fresh parsley
6 oz. can artichoke hearts, chopped

Depending on the occasion, I may add raisins, bite size pieces of cooked chicken, nuts etc.

Dressing:
1 C. mayonnaise (Hellmann's is my favorite)
½-1 tsp. curry powder
1 ½ - 2 tsp. turmeric
Juice of ½ lemon
½ tsp. paprika
Salt to taste

After mixing, pour over rice mixture, incorporate and chill – overnight is perfect.

COUSIN PENNY'S CAULIFLOWER/ BROCCOLI SALAD

Broccoli, cut up – use amt. desired
½ C. golden raisins
Cauliflower, cup up – use, amt. desired
8 slices bacon, fried crisp and broken up
½ C. sunflower seeds
Sweet red pepper strips, small cherry tomatoes
    (or any vegetable for color coordination)

Dressing:
1 C. Hellmann's mayonnaise
2 t.. Vinegar
¼ C. sugar

Pinch of salt
1 t. minced green onions

Mix and pour over vegetable mixture approximately ½ hour before serving.
Penny uses chopped cranberries instead of raisins at Christmas time making it
more festive looking.

GRILLED TUNA NICOISE PLATTER
Ála Ina Gartner

I once traveled from Florence, Italy to Paris, France by myself crying for an hour on a train which eventually broke down. I did not want to leave Italy, a country full of wonder for its food, history, art, music, romantic language, style, shoes, wines, cheeses and lovely people.

Nevertheless, I found my way to Paris, stopping just as a Madonna concert was exiting. Cabs were a premium and it was midnight. I do not speak French so I felt at a disadvantage. Staying at a small hotel which had a one person lift, I slept the night as well as the morning away from sheer exhaustion and missed the hotel's breakfast.

I followed the wonderful smells from an outdoor café and ordered salad nicoise because I knew how to pronounce it. Big Mistake! Much too much oil on an empty stomach. Still it was a lovely salad that I have made for special luncheon guests (sans the great amount of oil).

I took a cab to The Louvre where I was able to catch a quick look at the tiny Mona Lisa. Unfortunately, the salad oil began to upset my stomach and I had to tear around the art gallery, never too far from rest rooms.

Here, I offer a different marvelous grilled tuna nicoise platter recipe that allows each guest to make his/her own plate. It sounds complicated, but is not. It becomes a dish of tasty beauty,

INGREDIENTS (for 8)

8 (1 inch thick) fresh tuna steaks (about 4 pounds) – if you use canned tuna, which is much less expensive, be sure it has been packed in water.
Good extra virgin olive oil
Kosher salt and freshly ground black pepper
¾ pound French string beans, steams removed and blanched
1 recipe French Potato Salad, recipe follows
1 pounds ripe tomatoes, cut into wedges (6 small tomatoes)
8 hard-cooked eggs, peeled and cut in half
½ pound pitted black olives
1 bunch watercress or arugula
1 can anchovies (optional)   (Recipe continued on next page)

FOR THE VINAIGRETTE:

3 T. champagne vinegar
½ t. Dijon mustard   ¼ t. ground black pepper
½ t. kosher salt   10 T. good olive oil

DIRECTIONS

If using fresh tuna, grill it on a stove-top grill that is very hot. Brush the fish with olive oil, and sprinkle with salt and pepper. Grill each side for only 1 ½ to 2 minutes. The center should be raw like sushi or the tuna will be tough and dry... Arrange the tuna, green beans, potato salad, tomatoes, eggs, olives, watercress or arrugula and anchovies, if used on a larger flat platter.

FOR THE POTATO SALAD (added to the tuna nicoise on the platter)

1 pound small white boiling potatoes   2 T. good dry white wine
¾ t. freshly ground pepper   10 T. good olive oil ¼ cup minced
1 pound small red boiling potatoes   scallions
                                         (white and green parts)
2 T. chicken stock   2 T. minced fresh dill
2 T. champagne vinegar   ½ t. Dijon mustard
2 T. minced flat-leaf parsley   2 t. kosher salt
2 T. julienne fresh basil leaves

Drop the small red and white potatoes in a large pot of boiling salted water and cook for 20 to 30 minutes, until they are just cooked through. Drain in a colander and place a towel over the potatoes to allow then to steam for 10 more minutes. As soon as you can handle them, cut in ½ (quarters if they are larger) and place in a medium bowl. Toss gently with the wine and chicken stock. Allow the liquids to soak into the warm potatoes before proceeding.

Combine the vinegar, mustard, ½ teaspoon salt, and ¼ teaspoon pepper and slowly whisk in the olive oil to make an emulsion. Add the vinaigrette to the potatoes. Add the scallions, dill, parsley, basil, 1 ½ teaspoons salt and ½ teaspoon pepper and toss. Serve warm or at room temperature.

GERMAN COLE SLAW

1 C. white vinegar
½ t. salt
1 t. mustard
1 t. celery seed

¾ C. oil
1 cabbage, knife shredded
½ C. sugar
2 onions, thinly sliced

Layer cabbage and onion in large bowl and sprinkle sugar over mixture. Do not stir. Combine first 4 ingredients and boil for 1 minute and them add oil. Bring to boil again and pour over cabbage and onion. Do not stir. Cover and refrigerate at least 4 hours before serving. Keeps about 2 weeks.

GERMAN POTATO SALAD

Actually I extracted this recipe from the Kalamazoo Junior League Cookbook in 1978 because it was without doubt the best German potato salad I had ever found. I made it a gazillion times throughout the years and always got raves. . . . .and always at Christmas.

12 medium to large red potatoes (do not use baking potatoes – they break up)
1 # bacon
1 large onion, chopped
1 C. water
Salt and pepper to taste
1 pint sour cream (this is the kicker in this recipe)

1/8 C. white vinegar
¼ C. brown sugar, packed
½ t. celery seed

Boil potatoes with skins on until done, but still firm. Cool. I leave the skins on and cut them into ¾ inch pieces. Fry bacon until crisp and drain on paper toweling. After it cools, crumble it. Pour off all but 1/3 cup of bacon grease and add onion and cook slowly until tender. Add water, vinegar and sugar and simmer slowly over low heat for 5 minutes. Add potatoes and crumbled bacon to the mixture. Cover and cook over low heat for 15 minutes. Add celery seed, salt and pepper. Stir in sour cream.

CABBAGE SALAD
Ála Patti Volkel nee Rowan

I am so happy that I have this recipe from a fabulous cook who just stood in the kitchen and cooked and stirred. She was a friend from many years ago who recently passed away. As Irish as they come, she would put green food coloring in the cream of wheat and milk for her family on St. Patrick's Day morning and then get into the Bailey's Irish Crème the rest of the day, but have an Irish fare on the table come dinner time.

2 quarts shredded cabbage
2 chopped green peppers
1 chopped red pepper
4 medium or 2 large chopped onions

Boil:
1 pint vinegar
2 ½ C. sugar
½ t. turmeric
1 ½ t, salt
½ t. celery seed
1 ½ t. mustard seed

Pour boiled mixture over cabbage while hot. Put into refrigerator for 12 hours. Will keep for 2 weeks.

ANTIPASTO PLATTER

12 slices hard crusted round Italian break
   or 24 slices French bread (1/2 inch thick)
2 cloves garlic
12 slices prosciutto or thinly sliced fully cooked ham (about 6 ounces) cut in half
12 slices provolone cheese (about ¾ pound) cut in half
24 thin slices Genoa salami (about ¾ pound)
24 marinated mushrooms
24 marinated artichoke hearts
1/3 C. extra virgin olive oil or ½ c. vegetable oil
1 T. chopped fresh or 1 1/2 t. dried oregano leaves

If using Italian bread, cut each slice in half. Slather with butter   Cut each garlic clove in half; rub cut slides over both sides of bread. Toast in oven on both sides Arrange bread and remaining ingredients except oil, lemon and oregano on serving platter. Drizzle with oil. Squeeze juice from lemon over top and sprinkle with oregano.

EASY TACO DINNER (SALAD)

The Brey brothers, Hal and Jarl, had to endure my many makings of this during my coming out in Mexican cooking. Thank goodness it was tasty, but they never did say anything about the many repeat performances. . . and I would embellish and embellish.

1 pound ground beef
1 large onion, chopped
1 envelope Taco seasoning mix
1-12 oz. package tortilla chips

½ head lettuce, shredded
2 med. Tomatoes, chopped
1 C. shredded cheese
2/3 C. sour cream

Brown beef and onion in skillet, Stir in seasoning mix and water listed on package. Heat to boiling. Reduce heat and simmer for 10 minutes, stirring occasionally. Spoon mixture onto chips. Top with remaining ingredients. I have added peanuts, corn, and black beans . . . . Anything that goes with this winning fare.

COUSIN MARGO'S SAUERKRAUT SALAD

Margo writes that his salad has only 54 calories per cup (my kind of fare) and it keeps a good long time in frig.

1 large can or jar of sauerkraut
2 finely cut onions
1 green pepper, cut fine
1 C. celery, cut fine
1 large can Chinese bean sprouts
1 C. vinegar
Artificial sweetener to equal 1 ½ C. sugar
Add little salt and pepper

Boil all this together for about 5 minutes – let stand overnight in frig.
Keep unused portions in refrigerator.

. . . and HER WALDORF SALAD

½ C. mayonnaise
¼ t. ground allspice
1 C. celery, diced
1/3 C. chopped walnuts
3 T. lemon juice
2 C, diced chicken breasts
2 Granny Smith apples, cored/diced
1 T. sugar
1 C. red seedless grapes, halved
Salt and pepper to taste

Blend mayo, lemon juice, sugar and allspice. Add chicken, grapes, celery and apples. Season to taste with salt and pepper. Sprinkle with walnuts. Cover and refrigerate.

You might try adding cubed cheddar cheese or canned pineapple chunks for added flavor.

CRANBERRY SALAD

Dissolve: 1 pkg. cherry Jell-o
1 C. boiling water
1 C. sugar
1 T. lemon
1 C. pineapple juice

Add: 1 C. crushed pineapple
1 C. raw cranberries
1 orange - ground
1 C. celery, diced
½ C. chopped nuts

AMBROSIA – Jell-O Salad

When brother, Mack was living in Atlanta, I would visit him and lavish in all of the excitement. One year he and his wife even threw a party in my honor. It was a brunch and one of the things that was served was this recipe brought over by their next door neighbor, Mrs. Shearer, in a silver bowl, adorned beautifully. I was always impressed with the graciousness of southern living.

1 pkg. orange jell-O
1/3 C. sugar
1 C. boiling water
1 – 8 oz. can crushed pineapple
1 C. sour cream
¼ t. vanilla
1 can Mandarin oranges
½ C. coconut

Dissolve jell-O and sugar in water. Add pineapple juice. Refrigerate until partially set. Add sour cream and vanilla, whip until fluffy. Stir in other in other ingredients. Chill.

SEVEN LAYER SALAD

½ medium head lettuce, shredded
½ C. coarsely cut celery
½ C. coarsely cut red or green pepper
¾ C. coarsely cut Spanish onion
½ package frozen green peas, cooked
    slightly and drained

1 cup mayonnaise
1 ½ cups shredded mild cheddar cheese
4 strips bacon crips-cooked and broken

In a large salad bowl, arrange lettuce, celery, peppers, onion and peas in layers. Spread mayo evenly over peas. Sprinkle with cheddar cheese. Cover and refrigerate at least 4 hours or overnight. Sprinkle with bacon just before serving. Makes 6 servings.

FROZEN FRUIT SALAD

1 pkg. (3 0z.) cream cheese
1/3 C. mayo
2 T. lemon juice
Dash of salt
½ C. heavy cream, whipped
1 can (1# 14 oz.) fruit cocktail drained
1 C. diced bananas
¼ C. chopped pecans or walnuts
2 # diced maraschino cherries

Combine cream cheese, mayo, lemon juice, and salt in large bowl. Fold in whipped cream. Add fruit cocktail, bananas, nuts and cherries, mix well. Pour into loaf pan and pop into the freezer for 3 to 4 hours or until very firm. Slice for serving and place on a piece of lettuce. – 6-8 servings

FRENCH DRESSING by Pat Shorey, Eppinga, Goede

Blend ¼ C. vinegar, ½ C. sugar. Add one grated onion, minced. 1 t. salt. and paprika. Blend very well with 2/3 C. catsup, 1 C. olive oil. Add celery salt, then bleu cheese.

Note: To blend, use electric blender. For minced onions, use instant minced onions.

BASIC OIL AND VINEGAR DRESSING

You can play with this using flavored vinegars or wines. Use extra virgin olive oil.

½ C. olive oil   ½ t. salt
3 T. vinegar or wine of your choice   dash pepper, paprika

MEMPHIS CREAMY COLE SLAW

Mack and Mary Margrave sent a few additions for the Margrave Cookbook. This is a favorite salad of theirs.

½ C. mayonnaise
2 T. dill or sweet pickle juice
½ t. sugar
½ t. Lemon-Pepper seasoning
¼ t. salt
4 -5 C. packaged shredded cabbage with carrots (coleslaw mix)
½ C. chopped red onion

(double or triple ingredients as needed) The basic one serves 4-6.

In large bowl mix mayonnaise, pickle juice, sugar, lemon-pepper seasoning, salt. Stir in coleslaw mix and onion. Toss to coat. Cover and chill one hour before serving.

MOLDED LIME SALAD WITH ALMONDS

This is a great holiday salad to be served with turkey or ham.

Family-size lime jello
1 C. boiling water
½ t. salt
1 C. sour cream
½ C. sliced almonds
½ C. celery, finely sliced
1 #2 can crushed pineapple, drained

In a good sized bowl, dissolve Jello and salt into the boiling water. Add sour cream and mix well. Add remaining ingredients and stir, stir, stir. Put into a fun mold and let the refrigerator do the chilling over night.

MANDARIN ORANGE FLUFF

This is a recipe that was handed to me at one of the Duff family gatherings where everyone licked the disk clean because it was sooooo good. My cousin, Margo, asked for it when she was wintering in Florida and needed something easy to take to a potluck. She claimed that no less than **12** people begged for the recipe following the luncheon. Here it is – do enjoy!

1 pkg. tapioca pudding (lg. and not instant)
1 box vanilla pudding—lg.
1 box orange Jello—lg.
1 can drained mandarin oranges – lg.
2 C. water
1 container Cool Whip

In a pan, place the first three items and add the water using a whisk. Heat on low until thickened, stirring constantly. Remove from heat and cool. Fold in the Cool Whip and oranges. Refrigerate until ready to serve.

Notes

APPETIZERS & LIBATIONS

MOCK BOURSIN AU POIVRE

One Christmas, I gave this recipe in saved jars placing colorful material tied with tiny ribbons to hold the added attraction in place. I am not saying this is a great recipe but it was a great hit with the recipients. One was known to say, "I wanted to lick the jar clean when I couldn't get anymore out with a knife."

1-8 oz. package cream cheese
1 t. caraway seed
1 t. dill
Lemon pepper

1 Clove garlic, crushed
1 t. basil
1 t. chives, chopped

Blend together all ingredients but lemon pepper; shape into a ball and roll in the lemon pepper until covered. Refrigerate a day or more to blend flavors. Serve with plain wafers,

SHRIMP MOUSSE

I bought a special fish mold to congeal this and used sliced green olives for the eyes.

1 Envelope unflavored gelatin
¼ C. cold water
1 Can (10 ¾ oz) tomato soup
1- 8 oz. pkg. cream cheese
½ Green pepper, finely chopped
½ C. onion, finely chopped
½ C. celery, finely chopped
1 C. mayonnaise (I prefer Hellmann's)
2 Cans (6 ½ oz. each) small shrimp, drained

Dissolve gelatin in ¼ cup cold water, set aside. Combine soup (undiluted) and cream cheese, warm over low heat until melted. Add gelatin mixture. Set aside and cool. Mix green pepper, onion, celery, mayonnaise, and shrimp into the soup-gelatin mixture. Transfer into a fun mold. Refrigerate for at least 2 hours. Serve with plain crackers.

LA GUMBA

Whether the restaurant still exists, I know not, but this recipe was always at the salad bar and it sticks in my head. I have recently made it for a graduation party which I catered . . . It was devoured in nothing flat.

Frozen peas, thawed and drained
Spanish peanuts
Hellman's mayonnaise

In a mixing bowl, combine all ingredients and chill for at least 2 hours.

QUICK HORS D'OEUVER

Franks – use cocktail franks or cut up regular size franks
Sauce Mimosa - below
Toothpicks

Sauce Mimosa:
> ½ C. prepared mustard (your choice)
> ½ C. grape jelly
> 1 ½ T. lemon juice

Heat sauce and let simmer with franks in it for 5 minutes. Serve warm with toothpicks.

RITA REETZ'S MARINATED SHRIMP

This is one of those a little of this, a little of that recipe which her daughter, Petie Brey, gave me many years ago. Just start throwing in the ingredients and the end result will be wonderful.

Cooked, shelled, deveined shrimp
Oil
Vinegar
Sliced onion rings
Capers and juices

Celery seed
Salt and pepper
Bay leaves
Dash of Tabasco

Place in a large bowl, cover and marinate in refrigerator for 24 hours

CRACKER SPREAD

In the 1960s, they dared to say ...."Men love this"!

½ Lb. Swiss cheese, shredded
1 Small sweet onion, chopped a lot
Hellmann's mayonnaise, enough to moisten the mixture

Mix the above 3 ingredients together, top with a little fresh flat leaf parsley that has been chopped and place in a bowl on a plate that has some great crackers laid on it.

"PHILLY" MIRACLE WHIP WREATH

2 8-Oz. pkgs. Philadelphia Brand cream cheese softened
½ C. Miracles Whip Salad Dressing (I use Hellmann's Mayo)
1/3 C.(1 ½ oz.) Kraft Grated Parmesan cheese
10 Crispy cooked bacon slices, crumbled
¼ C. green onion, sliced
Nabisco Triscuit Wafers

Combine cream cheese and salad dressing, mixing until well blended. Add remaining ingredients; mix well. Chill.   Place drinking glass in center of serving platter. Drop rounded Tablespoons of mixture to form a ring around glass. Just touching outer edge of glass; smooth with spatula. Remove glass. Garnish with chopped parsley and pimiento just before serving if desired. (Go around top with parsley which accentuates the wreath and make a "ribbon" with the pimiento. It's quite lovely for the holidays at Christmas. Serve with waters.

SALMON MOUSSE LOAF

FILLIING:

1 – 1 lb. can red salmon (drained and rinsed)   1 T. finely chopped parsley
1 – 8 oz. pkg. cream cheese (softened)   2 Green onions (finely chopped)
½ C. sour cream; 1 t. lemon juice   1 t. worchestershire sauce
2 t. horseradish; 1 T. chili sauce   Salt and pepper to taste.

FROSTING:

1 – 8 oz. cream cheese, softened
2 – 3 T. sour cream

BREAD: 18 – Slices thin rye or darker bread. Cut off crusts.
Combine all Filling Ingredients. I use a mixer, you want this very fluffy.
Lay down 3 slices of bread alongside each other, then cover with filling.
Add a second slice and so on. Finish with bread.

Apply a thin layer of frosting on the loaf to seal – chill 1 hour.
Then spread remaining Frosting. Chill over night. Slice with wet knife. Garnish

AUNTIE GREET'S APPETIZER RIBS

3 to 4 pounds Country Style Spare Ribs, cut in individual portions. Put a little salt and pepper on ribs. Place in slow cooker with 2 cups of water. Cook on low for 6 to 7 hours or until tender. Drain. Arrange ribs on broiler pan and cover with sauce.

Sauce:

½ C. ketchup
2 T. vinegar
2 T. brown sugar

¼ T. salt
½ bottle steak sauce
1 T. minced onion

HOT CRABMEAT APPETIZERS

3- 8 Oz. pkgs. cream cheese
3 Cans crab meat (15 oz of imitation can also be used, but chop, chop, chop)
½ C. mayo
1 t. prepared mustard
Dash garlic salt
1 t. onion juice
2 t. confectioner's sugar sugar
4 Crackers, crushed
½ C. dry white wine

Mix all ingredients. Heat in a double boiled and transfer to a chafing dish for serving. Triscuits are a good accompaniment, but any kind of cracker may be served.

CHEESE THINGS

Blend 1 ¼ sticks butter and 8 Oz. extra sharp shredded cheddar cheese.

Mix in 1 C. sifted flour, 1 ½ C. slightly crushed corn flakes, 1 – 2 drops Tabasco, ¼ C. chopped nuts (any kind).

Drop by teaspoon on cookie sheet with waxed paper. Flatten a bit with fork. Bake at 350 for 15 minutes.

STUFFED MUSHROOMS PARMA

1 Lb. fresh mushrooms
½ C. (2 oz.) grated parmesan cheese
¼ C. butter, melted
1 T. chopped green onion

Remove stems of mushrooms, chop stems. Combine stems, cheese, butter and onion. Fill mushroom caps. Place on rack of broiler pan; broil 2 – 3 minutes or until top of filling is slightly crusty. Serve hot.

DOUGLAS BOARDWELL, THE FIRST's BACON WRAPS

1 Lb. bacon, cut in half   2 Cans whole water chestnuts, drained

Sauce:

1 C. catsup   1 Jar peach baby food
6 T. sugar   Dash of hot sauce or lemon juice (if desired)

Wrap bacon around water chestnuts, secure with a toothpick. Slide into a 375 degree oven until bacon is browned. Keep a close eye on these. Mix all sauce ingredients and pour over hot bacon wrapped water chestnuts. Serve.

PIZZA ON A CRACKER

1 Lb. hot sausage
1 Lb. learn ground beef
1 T. oregano
½ t. garlic salt
1 Lb. Velveeta cheese
Party crackers

Meat should be browned. After draining off grease, add seasoning and cheese. Spread on crackers and heat in 400 degree oven for 15 minutes.

TASTES LIKE PIZZA SNACK

Pat Hess, Shorey, Eppinga, Goede shared the wonderful recipes she brought back from the east side of the state when she visited family. Her sister was very up on what was new and different in the culinary world. Here is one that was a real winner when I entertained.

1 Package of very mini rye bread (get it in the deli department)
1 C. Parmesan cheese (in the shake container)
3 C. Hellmann's mayonnaise
½ small onion grated on finest sieve
Fry 10 slices of bacon and crumble
1 Jar green olives with pimentos

Mix the mayo and cheese together, add the bacon (I never used bacon, but I am typing what the recipe says). Slather the mixture onto the mini rye bread and top with slices of olives. Toast in a 450 degree oven. Watch them carefully just until they bubble.

LIVERSAUSAGE CREAM CHEESE SPREAD

1 Lb.. liversausage
¼ C. mayonnaise
2 T. dill pickle juice
1 T. worcestershire sauce

3 drops Tabasco
¼ T. garlic salt
8 Oz. cream cheese, softened
1/3 C. finely chopped dill pickles

Mash liversausage with fork, beat until smooth, add mayonnaise, pickle juice, worchestershire sauce, garlic salt, Tabasco and 1/3 of the cream cheese. Blend until smooth, stir in chopped pickle. Line a deep bowl with plastic wrap, pack mixture into bowl. Leave several hours. Turn onto tray, frost with remaining softened cream cheese. Chill at least 2 hours. I used to throw a little chopped parsley on the top for effect.

SUE D'S CHEESE BALL

Sue Duff was my quilting mentor. I met her in my second quilting class where there were three Sues. She had a very uppity machine which did everything including whistling Dixie and when someone called for Sue, three heads turned. She then become Sue D. to me and has been an incredible friend for many years now. Somehow I got talked into making all of the food for her granddaughter's high school graduation party, (I was caterer for a day and really enjoyed it) but Sue D. produced this little gem and I share it with you.

2-8 oz. packages of cream cheese
1- 8 oz package of shredded cheddar cheese
1 small can drained pineapple

2 T. chopped green onion
2 t. Worcestershire sauce

Mix these 5 ingredients; form into a ball, chill. Roll in 2/3 cup chopped walnuts.

SHRIMP CHEESE BALL

Another of Lucille MaGill's contributions.

2-Pkg. 3 oz. cream cheese, softened
Blend in 1 ½ t, prepared mustard
1 t. grated onion

1 Dash cayenne
1 Dash salt
1 ½ Oz can shrimp, drained

Mix together and add 1 dash horseradish. Roll and chill. Roll in chopped salted mixed chopped nuts. Serve with crackers.

CRABMEAT CHEESE BALL

2- 8 oz. pkgs. cream cheese mixed with horseradish to taste.
1 Package frozen crabmeat (or may use 2 pkg. imitation which should be
      chopped).
Sauce: ketchup and horseradish to taste
Pour over crabmeat ball and serve with assorted crackers

Note: I have also plunked a brick of cream cheese on a pretty serving plate and put either red or green pepper jelly over it.

COUSIN PENNY AND HER MOTHER, AUNT LORNA ADAMS LANOUETTE'S CHEESE BALL

1 Stick butter
1 C. Rice Krispies
2 C. flour
Few shakes dry mustard
1 C. grated sharp cheese

Mix all together and form into balls the size of marbles. Put on a parchment paper surface covering a cookie sheet and bake 20 minutes at 350 degrees.

BLUE CHEESE BALL

8 Oz. blue cheese, crumbled
8 Oz. cream cheese, softened
1 C. cheddar cheese, grated
8 oz. pineapple tidbits, drained
½ t. seasoned salt
1 T. Worcestershire sauce
1 C. pecans, chopped
1 C. fresh parsley, minced

Combine all ingredients, except parsley in a bowl and mix well. Form into a ball shape and roll in minced parsley. Chill for 1 hour before serving with crackers. The blue cheese adds interesting flavor to the traditional cheese ball. Also, rolling the ball in parsley rather than nuts makes for a different presentation.

HAM APPETILLAS

1 pkg. Azteca Super Size Flour Tortillas
2 – 8 oz. pkg. cream cheese, softened
1/3 C. mayo
2 T. green onion, chopped
¼ C. black olives, chopped
2 – 2 ½ oz. pkg. sliced, pressed, cooked ham

Remove tortillas from refrigerator. Combine cream cheese, mayo, onions, and olives. Spread thin mixture on tortilla. Arrange 4 slices of ham over cheese. Tightly roll up tortilla. Wrap individually in plastic wrap. Place in refrigerator at least 3 hours or over night. To serve, cut into ¾ inch slices. Makes about 64 appetillas Note: Omit olives and ham. Add ¼ cup chopped red pepper, 1 cup shredded cheddar cheese and 1 can of crab, drained (5 oz. imitation crab) to mixture.

TRADITIONAL PARTY MIX RECIPE

½ C. butter
1 ¼ t. seasoned salt
4 ½ t. Worcestershire sauce
2 C. Corn Chex cereal
2 C. Rice Chex cereal
2 C. Bran Chex cereal
2 C. Wheat Chex cereal
2 C. salted mixed nuts

Preheat oven to 250. Heat butter in large shallow roasting pan (about 15x10x2) in oven until melted. Remove. Stir in seasoned salt and Worcestershire sauce. Add Chex and nuts. Mix until all pieces are coated. Heat in oven 1 hour. Stir every 15 minutes. Spread on absorbent paper to cool. Makes about 9 cups
Helpful hint: Party Mix may be frozen, so you can save time when you make a double batch. Thaw at room temperature in container in which it was stored.

LIVER PASTE

Another great recipe from Pat Shorey, Eppinga, Goede.

In a frying pan:
Melt ¼ C. of butter plus ½ C. of butter
½ Clove garlic, minced or 1/8 t. garlic powder
3 Medium onions, finely chopped
Fry until tender and soft but not brown.
Then add 1 Lb. chicken livers, washed and drained. Cook slowly until tender.

In blender:
2 Sprigs or ½ t. parsley flakes, flat leaved
1 ½ t. salt
½ t. Tabasco sauce
¼ t. ground cloves
2 T. white wine or sherry

Then blend ½ chicken liver mixture at a time. Let it chill overnight or at least 4 hours. Serve with crackers..

ANOTHER WINNING LIVER PASTE

(the news paper from which this recipe came is yellow with age).

¼ C. butter
1 Lb. chicken livers, washed and drained
1 ½ C. finely chopped onions
1 t. salt
¼ t. dry mustard
¼ t. freshly ground black pepper
¼ t. powdered thyme
Dash mace
¼ C. cream

1. Heat butter in skillet over medium heat; add chicken livers and onion and cook stirring frequently, about 8 minutes or until livers are done and onion is tender but not brown.
2. Force liver with onion through a strainer or spin in a blender; blend in seasonings and cream and turn into serving container or mold. Chill thoroughly and serve with thinly sliced French bread, crackers or toast rounds. Makes 1 1/3 cups.

SPINACH BALL APPETIZERS

2 Pkg. frozen chopped spinach (10 oz size)
2 C. herbed stuffing mix (packaged)
1 C. grated parmesan cheese
1 Egg beaten
¾ C. softened butter
Salt and pepper to taste

Cook spinach according to package directions and drain well, squeeze. Combine all ingredients and roll into walnut size balls. Place on cookie sheets and enfold tightly with foil. Freeze. When ready to use, place the frozen balls on another cookie sheet and bake about 10 minutes at 350. Makes 60 to 70 balls.

SPINACH PUFFS

1- 12 oz. package of Stouffer's Spinach soufflé, defrosted (microwave
              50% for 6-7 min)
¾ C. all purpose flour
1 t. baking powder
½ t. salt
1 Slightly beaten egg
¾ t. dehydrated minced onion
¾ C. Swiss cheese shredded
¼ C. toasted bread crumbs
Parmesan cheese in a container

Sift flour, baking powder and salt together. Combine Spinach Souffle and beaten egg; add flour mixture; stir in remaining ingredients and blend thoroughly. Refrigerate ½ hour. Heat 2 inches of corn oil in a sauce pan to 350 degrees. Drop batter by Tablespoons into hot oil. Fry 2 minutes or until golden brown. Remove and drain on paper towel. Dust with Parmesan cheese. Serve hot.

CANDIED GINGER DIP

-- one of my favorites

Mary Lou Green gave me this recipe when she was a young bride in the 1970's She already had the makings of a wonderful cook and great homemaker.

Mix together: 1 C. Hellmann's mayo
              1 C. sour cream
              ¼ C. onion, finely chopped
              ¼ C. fresh parsley, snipped
              1 Can water chestnuts, cut fine
              1 T. candied ginger, cut very fine
              1 T. soy sauce
After mixing well, refrigerate, cover for at least 4 hours or over night

VEGETABLE PIZZA

When granddaughter, Elyse, was a student at The Gagie School in Kalamazoo, Michigan, she seemed to enjoy cooking with me. I think that she also may have had dreams of becoming an actress. so when I was asked to do a cooking show (just one) for one of the people who worked at Barnes and Noble for local TV, she decided that would be a great project for her to do with her "DD" (that's me). We thought we had 'arrived'. Together we cooked and sputtered our way through 5 dishes in ½ hour. One of the offerings we made is as follows:

2 Pkg. crescent rolls
2 (8 Oz.) pkgs. cream cheese
2/3 C. mayonnaise (Hellmann's)
1 Pkg, Hidden Valley mix
½ C. sour cream
1 T. sugar

1 C. green onions, sliced thin
1 C. celery, chopped
1 C. carrots, cut
1 C. cheese, shredded

+ other veggies, like chopped broccoli, chopped cauliflower, or any of your favorites

Roll your crescent roll on an ungreased cookie sheet. Bake 10minutes at 350 degrees. Mix together cream cheese, mayonnaise, Hidden Valley mix sour cream and sugar. Spread on cooled crescent rolls and top with vegetables.

COUSIN MARGO'S VEGETABLE DIP

Combine the following ingredients together. Chill several hours before serving.

1 C. sour cream
1 C. mayonnaise
1 T. parsley flakes
1 T. dried onions
1 t. Beau Monde

½ t. garlic salt
1 t. Accent seasoning
2 Drops Tabasco sauce
2 t. Dill weed

TEX-MEX LAYERED DIP

Maria Cassidy Spielmacher entertained our bridge bunch one warm summer evening in the back yard of her East Grand Rapids home. The guest list included the 4 regulars plus the substitutes (it seems no one plays Bridge anymore, but we had a lot of fun throughout the years and gained lifelong friends) The number consisted of us 4, 2 subs plus husbands, dates, mates and significant others. We were introduced to this recipe and it was gobbled up, so I offer it to you. Be creative if you need to substitute.

1 15 oz can black beans, rinsed and drained
2 T. Old el Paso Thick 'n Chunky Salsa
1 ½ C. sour cream
1 C. guacamole
1 C. shredded cheddar cheese
1 Small tomato, seeded and chopped – about ½ cup
2 Medium green onions, chopped
Tortilla chips

Mix black beans and salsa in a small bowl. Spoon into a circle on a 12-13 inch serving plate.

Spoon sour cream in center and smooth to within an inch of where the beans end.

Spoon guacamole in center of sour cream and spread to within an inch of where sour cream ends, leaving a border showing.

Sprinkle cheese, tomato and onions over guacamole. Cover with plastic wrap and refrigerate for up to 6 hours. Serve with tortilla chips.

FRESH SALSA

I worked with Lynda Petty who left education to enter the world of business. She and her husband Joe bought a Bed and Breakfast in Puerto Vallarta, Mexico. This comes from there and is a treat.

6 Roma tomatoes, chopped
1 Small onion, chopped
½ Small head cabbage, chopped
1 – 2 Sarona peppers, finely chopped
1 t. salt
½ t. pepper
½ t. sugar
1 t. ground celery seed
1 t. chopped cilantro

Combine the ingredients in a medium bowl and blend until well mixed. Refrigerate until serving

DEBRA BOARDWELL COLBY'S CHEESE AND CHILI DIP

Deb is twin to Cindy and the eldest of the Boardwell kids.

4 Cans no-bean chili
1 Medium size brick of Velveeta cheese
1 Lb. ground beef

Cook ground beef and crumble like taco meat. Add chili. Cube cheese, add all ingredients and put in a microwave bowl. Microwave until cheese is melted, stirring often. Serve with a bag of tortilla or corn chips.

HOT DIP

Mac and Lucille MaGill were wonderful neighbors of mine when I lived in the house on Radcliff. They were almost like parents. Mac adored our dog, Ralph Bunch, and once rescued him from death at the pound after he had chased a lovely lady dog far beyond our neighborhood. We were eternally grateful! They are all gone now — Lucille, Mac and Ralph Bunch — but I think about them often with very fond memories. Lucy shared this recipe with me and so I share it with you.

8 oz. cream cheese
2 T. milk
2 T. chopped green peppers
1 pkg. chipped beef

¼ C. sour cream
2 T. minced onion flakes
1/8 t. pepper
¼ C. walnuts.

Bake 15 minutes at 350. Serve with crackers

GUACAMOLE

When eldest son, Hal, was graduating from high school and ready to start his studies at Purdue, I threw him a party. Per his request, we served guacamole before it was well known and he thought that he had arrived. He was an early gourmand!

1 large or 2 small avocados, peeled, chopped
½ Small onion, chopped
1 Clove garlic, crushed
1 T. lemon juice
½ t. salt
1 Can (4 oz.) roasted peeled green chilies

Put ingredients in a food processor and blend to desired consistency. Refrigerate. Serve with Doritos. Variations: Add a tomato, peeled and chopped, several sprigs coriander, and a pinch of sugar. You may use this as a topping for omelets, tacos, nachos and salads

DILL CHIP DIP

- another anonymous student's gift to me

Mix a day ahead and refrigerate, covered:

> 1 t. dill weed
> 1 t. Beau Monde
> 1 t. parsley
> 1 T. grated onion
> 2/3 C. mayo
> 2/3 C. sour cream

COUSIN MARGO'S TACO CHEESE DIP

1 Large brick Velveeta cheese
1 Medium onion, diced
1 Large tomato, diced
1 Jar Ortega Taco Sauce
1 Pt. sour cream
1 to 2 Lbs. ground beef
1 Diced green pepper

Combine all ingredients and put in crock-pot at low temperature. When every-thing is melted together, serve over taco chips. Add green pepper, onions, to-mato and sour cream after first ingredients are melted together.

WHIPPED CREAM DIP FOR FRUIT – a la Lucille Magill

¼ C. mayo
1 T. sugar
½ t. lemon juice
Dash salt
½ C. whipping cream, whipped

DEBRA BREY'S HIDDEN VALLEY RANCH YOGURT DIP

16 oz. non-fat plain yogurt
1 Packet Hidden Valley Ranch Dressing (dry mix)
2 T. non-fat mayo
Pinch of Equal

Mix yogurt and mayo. Add dry Hidden Valley mix and mix well. Add small amt. of Equal to take off edge of yogurt's sharp taste. Refrigerate. Says Debra, "This dip is great for baked potatoes, vegetable dip and salad dressing or as a substitute for mayo in tuna or chicken salads".

FRESH CORN TOMATO SALSA

1 C. fresh corn, cooked (I use frozen)
1 Large ripe tomato, peeled, seeded and chopped
1 Small cucumber; peeled, seeded and chopped
1 Small onion, finely chopped
1 Small celery stalk, chopped
1 Jalapeño pepper, chopped
3 T. lime juice, freshly squeezed
½ t. cumin
1 Large garlic clove, minced
½ t. salt
1 T. sugar

In a medium bowl, stir together all ingredients until mixed well. Cover and refrigerate, allowing flavors to blend for at least an hour.

ROASTED GARLIC

Slice the top half–inch from 4 whole heads of garlic. Remove some of the papery skins from the outside, keeping the head intact. Place in a baking dish, drizzle each with 1 T. olive oil and sprinkle with salt and pepper. Cover and bake for 1 hour in a 275 degree oven. Uncover, baste with the oil in the dish and sprinkle each with 1 T. grated Parmesan cheese. Cove and bake 1 more hour or until tender. Serve warm by squeezing garlic cloves out of their skins onto crisp crackers or sliced, fresh bread and spreading with a knife. Serves 4-6.

MY MAMA'S CRANBERRY MEATBALLS

Cousin Penny asked for this recipe and I was so afraid that it had got lost in the shuffle of my many moves. I am a semi-gypsy and have come and gone many times. I am very happy where I now reside in my very old condo where I continually use my interior design skills in Kalamazoo (yes, Alice, there is a Kalamazoo) and travel to faraway lands when the Eagle lands. I hunted and hunted, dear cuz, and so here it is. Thanksgiving for the family would be a wonderful time to serve this!

2 Lbs. ground beef
1 C. corn flakes
1/3 C. parsley
2 eggs
½ C. catsup

1 T. soy sauce
½ t. garlic powder
2 T. onion, minced well
¼ t. pepper

Roll into balls and place in pan.

Sauce:
Heat 1 Can jell cranberry sauce
12 Oz bottle chili sauce
2 T. brown sugar
1 T. lemon juice
Cook until smooth, stirring occasionally
Bake at 300 for 1 hour uncovered.
I would think that a slow cooker on low might work as well.

YUMMY COCKTAIL MEAT BALLS

Elyse and I also made these on our TV debut with great flair. They are so good, even Parker, her youngest brother who eats nothing but mac- n –cheese devoured them.

1 Pkg. frozen meat balls (5 lbs.)
2 Jars (1 lb. ea.) chili sauce
1 Jar (14 oz.) grape jelly

Incorporate the jelly and chili sauce untill blended. Throw everything into a slow cooker on high for 3 hours or until meat balls have thawed and sauce is bubbling.

HOT DATE/ALMOND TREATS

Put the almonds inside the dates and wrap them with half of a slice of bacon which you have secured with a toothpick. Place in a 375 degree oven which you are watching carefully until bacon is done. The results are mouthwatering.

CRACKER SNACKS

1 Pkg. oyster crackers
1 Pkg. buttermilk ranch salad dressing dry mix
¼ t. lemon pepper
½ -1 t. dill weed
¼ t. garlic powder
¾ C. salad oil /vegetable oil

Mix dry dressings and oil together. Add dill, garlic powder and lemon pepper. Pour over crackers, stir to coat. Place in warm oven 300 degrees for 15 – 20 minutes.

3 CANAPE'S ALA COUSIN MARGO

<u>1. Rye Bread</u> - cut in circles or squares
    1 can deviled ham mixed with 1 T. Horseradish
Cover bread with above mixture and top with a slice of black or green olive or a tiny piece of sliced sweet or dill pickle.

<u>2. White bread</u> – cut in circles or squares
    Take one package of cream cheese and mix in a drained can of pineapple or mixed fruit – whip together. Spread on bread circles or squares and top with green or red maraschino cherries, sliced.

<u>3. Deviled Eggs</u>

Boil eggs, cook in pan of water, peel and slice in two.

Filling for 8 whole eggs (16 halves):
½ C. Mayonnaise
½ C. chopped black olives
2 T. chopped parsley
2 T. marjoram leaves
The egg yolks

Mash together and fill the empty egg halves

...... and Libations

HOT CHOCOLATE

2 Lbs. dry milk
8 Oz. of any coffee cream substitute

2 C. powdered sugar
2 Lbs. Nestle Quik

Mix together. Put ¼ cup mix in a cup. Fill with hot water

SPICED TEA

1 C. sugar
1 C. Tang
½ C. instant lemonade

½ C. instant tea
1 t. cinnamon
½ t. cloves

Mix all ingredients together. Store in a container. Use 2 teaspoons per cup of hot water for refreshing spiced tea.

SIMPLE COFFEE PUNCH

1 Gallon strong chilled coffee
2 Qts. coffee or chocolate ice cream
4 t. vanilla
1 Qt. whipping cream
¼ C. sugar

Put chilled coffee in punch bowl and stir in melting ice cream and vanilla, whip cream, add sugar, and fold into punch just before serving. Serves 30-35.

VODKA PUNCH

Peg Dangl was another favorite secretary. She was a great mom, loved to laugh and party. She was also a great cook and gatherer of new recipes. Here is her vodka punch:

1/5 Vodka
1 Can lemonade (use as directed)
1 Qt. bottle lemon-lime soda
Serve with an ice ring.

2 – Fifths of vodka makes 3 punch bowls – for a single bowl, use 2/3 of a fifth.

MOST FABULOUS COCOA IN THE WORLD

3 Oz. crème de cacao
1 ½ C. hot milk
Salt
1 Egg
Whipped cream

Combine everything but the whipped cream, beat well with egg beater. Ladle into mugs. Top with crème de cacao flavored whipped cream.

IRISH COFFEE

This was always on the fare when I went to Ireland . . . .anywhere and every-where in the wonderful pubs.

Hot coffee
1 Jigger (ounce) Irish whiskey in
   Irish coffee glass

½ t. sugar, or to taste
3 T. Cognac
Whipping cream, prepared

Fill glass ¾ full with hot coffee. Add Irish whiskey, sugar to taste, cognac and stir. Top with whipped cream. Sip!

CRANBERRY LIQUEUOR

Florence Obstfeld was my best gal pal when I lived in Portland, Oregon. She and I would drive through the city, she manning the map, I, driving. We inevitably got lost and laughed our heads off. I really miss her. Here is one of her recipies.

1-12 oz. package whole cranberries (about 4 cups) – can use frozen berries
2 ½ C. vodka or light rum
2 C. sugar
Strips of peel from 1 small orange

Rinse berries thoroughly. Coarsely chop berries and place in clean jar along with vodka or rum, sugar, and orange peel. Cover and store in cool dark place <u>for 3 months.</u> Shake and turn jar about every week to help dissolve sugar Strain carefully and bottle with tight-fitting cap or cork. Allow to age a month longer before using. Keep in freezer after made. – Yields about 4 cups

SLUSH PUNCH

Everyone loves this punch. It was served at my mom's 75the surprise birthday party. The recipe was given to me by a former colleague, Jerry Southland and his wife Shirley.

Make a simple syrup with 2-2 ½ C. sugar and 3 C. water

Add and mix together: 1 -12 oz. can frozen orange juice
                          1 12 oz can frozen lemonade
                          1 Large can pineapple juice
                          3 C water
Freeze in two 9x13 pans

Thaw for one hour and mix each pan with a two liter size bottle of 7-Up or Squirt. Perhaps some mint leaves might be added. Put in a punch bowl and ladle away

LIMONCELLO

After reading as well as watching, *UNDER THE TUSCAN SUN*, I madly searched for a recipe to make limoncello, a lemon liqueur prized by the Italians. I found one and gave it as Christmas gifts one year. Mixed reviews: my friend, Suzi Mittlesteadt raved and my youngest son, Jarl Brey chose not to use it and dumped it down the drain. Alas!

You may use it as a strait aperitif or mix it to make spritzers. I will add the spritzer recipe (a mixed version for the faint of heart) immediately following the limoncello directive. (This must be sipped)

10 Lemons
1 750-mil bottle of vodka
3 ½ C. of water
2 ½ C. sugar

Using a vegetable peeler, remove the peel from the lemons in long strips (reserve the lemons for another use). Using a sharp knife, trim away the white pith from the lemon peels discarding it. Place lemon peels in a two quart pitcher. Pour the vodka over the peels, cover with plastic wrap and let sit <u>for 4 days</u> at room temperature.

Stir the water and sugar in a large sauce pan over medium heat until sugar dissolves, about 5 minutes. Cool completely. Pour the sugar syrup over the vodka mixture. Cover and let stand overnight. Strain the limoncello through a mesh strainer. Discard the peels. Transfer the limoncello to bottles and refrigerate until cold, at least 4 hours or up to 1 month.

LIMONCELLO MINT SPRITZERS

2 C. limoncello
Coarsely crushed ice cubes
1 C. fresh mint leaves

1 C. club soda or lemon-lime soda
1 Lime, for garnish (optional)

1. Coarsely crush the ice cubes, and then fill 4 tall skinny drink glasses halfway full with the ice.
2. Add ¼ C. mint leaves to each glass and <u>using a muddle stick or the handle of a wooden spoon</u>, crush the mint leaves together with the ice (this is called "muddling").
3. Add ½ C. of limoncello to each glass, and stir.
4. Add ¼ C. of club soda to the top of each drink, and serve.
5. Quarter the lime for each glass so that guests may squeeze the juice into their spritzer.

SANGRIA

1 ½ C. lime or lemon juice
2 C. sugar
3 C. brandy or other dry red table wine
3 Pts. chilled club soda
Lime and orange slices

Combine lime juice, sugar and wine; stir until sugar is dissolved. Chill. Add club soda just before serving. Pour over ice. Float lime and orange slices in punch-bowl. Makes 2 ½ quarts.

WHITE SANGRIA

1 Gallon dry white wine (Gallo's white Zinfandel works fine)
2 C. orange juice, freshly squeezed
½ C. lime juice, freshly squeezed
½ C. lemon juice, freshly squeezed

¼ C. sugar
1 C. lemon-lime soda, chilled
Orange slices

Combine first 6 ingredients. To serve, add ice, garnish with orange slices. Yields 1 ¼ gallons

CHAMPAGNE SANGRIA

1 Bottle of Prosecco or French Champagne, chilled (Prosecco is Italian version)
½ C. orange juice
2 C. Mint Simple Syrup, recipe follows*
1 Lemon, zested and thinly sliced
1 Lime, zested and thinly sliced
½ C. sliced strawberries
5 Fresh mint sprigs
Crushed ice

In a large pitcher, combine the Prosecco, orange juice, Mint Simple Syrup* lemon zest and lime zest. Add the sliced strawberries, lemon slices and mint sprigs. Fill glasses with crushed ice and pour the sangria over the top. Serve immediately

*Mint Simple Syrup
2 C. sugar   2 C. water   1 C. packed fresh mint leaves

In a small saucepan, combine the sugar, water and mint over medium heat. Bring to a boil, reduce heat and simmer for 5 minutes, stirring occasionally, until the sugar has dissolved. Remove the pan from heat and allow the syrup to cool for 20 minutes. Strain before using.   Yields 2 ½ cups

WHISKEY SOURS

1 Can orange juice
1 Can lemonade
1 Can bourbon
1 Can water
Maraschino cherries
Crushed ice

Blender together, pour over crushed ice, throw in a cherry and be careful because they are power houses.

HOT SPICED WINE

Each Christmas Pat Hess, Shorey, Eppinga, Goede would deliver a bottle of this treasured wine which was a special delight after we had been cross country skiing. My mother got the recipe from her and I offer it to you.

1 Qt. water
3 C. sugar
12 whole cloves
4 inches stick cinnamon
6 whole allspice
½ t. ginger
Rind of 1 orange – grated
Rind of 1 lemon – grated
2 C. orange juice
1 C. lemon juice
1 Bottle California Burgundy

Combine all but juice and burgundy in sauce pan. Bring to a boil 'til sugar is dissolved – simmer for 10 minutes. Remove from heat – let stand 1 hour – strain and add juices and wine. To serve: Heat gently, Do Not Boil. Merry Christmas and Winter!

MAIN FARE

I LOVE MEAT LOAF! Either you love it or you hate it. To begin this part of my cookbook, I give you a plethora of different recipes I have found over the years.

CROCKPOT OR OVEN MEAT LOAT

This is a very easy and very good recipe and slices well for meatloaf sandwiches the next day.

2 Lb. lean ground beef
2 Eggs
2/3 C. Quaker Oats
1 Pkg. dry onion soup mix
½ C. catsup or barbecue sauce.

Reserve 2 Tb. Catsup. Combine beef, eggs, oats, soup mix and remaining catsup. Shape into a round loaf for crock-pot or oblong for oven. Put in crock pot or bread pan. Top with remaining catsup. Cover and cook on low 8-10 hours or 4-6 hours on high. If using oven, cook for about 1 hour 15 minutes at 350 degrees. Cover with foil if browning too fast.

EASY MEATLOAF

2 Lb. lean ground beef
1 Pkg. (6 oz.) Stove Top Stuffing Mix for Chicken
1 C. water
2 Eggs, beaten
1/2 C. Kraft Original Barbecue Sauce, divided

Heat oven to 375 degrees. Mix all ingredients except ¼ cup barbeque sauce. Shape meat mixture into oval loaf in 13 x 9 inch baking dish; top with remaining barbecue sauce.
Bake 1 hour or until done (160 degrees).

COUSIN PENNY'S SAVORY MEAT LOAF

2 Thin slices diced salt port
2 Lb. ground round steak
½ C. minute tapioca, uncooked
½ Onion - - chopped fine
2 C. canned tomatoes
2 t. salt - - ½ t. pepper

Fry out salt port until golden brown. Add with drippings to other ingredients. Mix thoroughly. Bake in loaf pan in hot oven (450) 15 minutes. Reduce heat to 350 and bake 30 minutes longer. (Editor's note: If you like green olives chop some up and throw those in to the mixture as well).

MEAT LOAF WELLINGTON

1 Egg, beaten
½ C. milk
1 C. tomato, skinned and diced
3 Slices white bread, crusts removed,
   and bread broken into ¼ " pieces
   (Give crusts to birds)
½ C. pine nuts   (chopped blanched almonds may be substituted)

1 C. celery, chopped
1 t. poultry seasoning
2 t. salt
¼ t. pepper
1-1/2 Lb. ground beef
¾ C. onion, chopped

Preheat oven to 375. Grease an 8 ½ "x 4 ½ "x 2 ½ " loaf pan. Combine egg, milk, and tomato, add bread cubes, onion, celery, seasonings, beef and nuts. Place in pan. Bake 1 hour 15 min. Cool and remove from pan. Freeze, if desired, but thaw before preparing Wellington topping.

Topping:
2 (10 Oz. each) pkgs. Frozen patty-shell
   pastry, thawed
½ C. mushrooms, sliced, and cooked

1 C. Cheddar cheese, shredded
1 Egg, beaten with 2 T. water
¼ C. green onions, chopped

(Continued on next page)

Preheat oven to 400. Use an ungreased baking sheet. Let pastry stand at room temperature about 15 min. Form into ball. Combine mushrooms onions, cheese

and spread on top of meatloaf. Roll out pastry 18" x 12". Wrap meat loaf. Use egg to seal loaf, also brush top and sides. Place on baking sheet and bake for 30 – 40 min. Let stand 10 minutes before carving. (Editor's note: Use some of the pastry to shape some small leaves that will puff up and look enticing).

TLC: Save bones and leftovers in a special place in the freezer and combine later for a sauce base.

GRATED CARROT MEAT LOAF FOR A CROWD

In 1985, I met the most wonderful young woman who had just finished her graduate education and was hired by The Forest Hills School System (east of Grand Rapids, MI) to teach special education. I had never met anyone who was as gifted, prepared or dedicated as Roxanne Gerds. She was from the east side of the state so I adopted her and she truly became the daughter I never had. We tried to cross stitch together but she sewed the thread to her sweatshirt. We tried knitting, but that didn't work either. So we said, " Fooey", and decided the greatest thing we did together was to eat and so we embarked on a great adventure for 30 years. She is one of my very favorite people and she so enjoyed this meat loaf recipe.

A mustard-flavored sugary glaze bakes on this carrot-flecked ground beef loaf.

2 Slices firm white bread, broken in pieces	2 T. prepared horseradish
¾ C. milk	1 Envelope onion soup mix
2 ½ Lb. lean ground beef	¼ C. catsup
3 Eggs	3 T. firmly packed brown sugar
2 Large carrots, finely shredded	2 T. Dijon mustard

Whirl bread in a blender to make about 1 cup fine crumbs. In a large mixing bowl, pour milk over bread crumbs and let stand until absorbed. Mix in ground beef, eggs, carrots, horseradish, and onion soup mix. Pat into a 9x5 inch loaf pan. Mix together catsup, brown sugar, mustard – spread evenly over top. 325-350 degrees for an hour.

MEAT LOAF FLORENTINE

Just one more of the meat loaf varieties and this is it!

1 pkg. frozen spinach (10 oz.)
½ C. celery, coarsely chopped
¼ C. milk
¾ Lb. ground beef
½ Lb. ground pork
1 t. ground pepper

¾ C. pitted ripe olives, coarsely chopped
½ C. frozen chopped onion
2 eggs lightly beaten
1 clove garlic, crushed
½ C. fresh bread crumbs
¾ t. salt and ¼ t. nutmeg

Defrost spinach. Drain very well. Pat dry with paper towel. Put celery and milk into electric blender and blend well. In large bowl, combine blended celery mixture and remaining ingredients, except tomato olive sauce. Mix together gently but thoroughly. Press mixture into a 6-cup ring mold or shape as a ring on a lightly greased baking sheet. Remove ring mold. Bake in a 350 degree oven for 1 to ¼ hours. Remove from oven. Serve with Sicilian tomato/olive sauce. Makes 6 to 8 servings.

Sicilian tomato/olive sauce

2 T. butter
1 C. frozen chopped onion
1 Can (14 oz.) Italian tomatoes
½ C. canned beef broth
1 Clove garlic, crushed

1 Bay leaf
½ t. basil
½ t. thyme
¼ t. sugar
1 C. pitted ripe olives, drained

Melt butter in saucepan. Add onion and cook until tender but not brown. Add remaining ingredients except the ripe olives. Cook sauce uncovered over low heat for about 45 minutes, stirring occasionally. Cut olives into small wedges. About 15 minutes before sauce is completed, stir in ripe olives. Makes 3 cups.

POTATO MEAT BALLS

This is a recipe from a Mrs. Johnson, but if you lived in Whitehall, MI, it was Mrs. Yon-son

1 Lb. ground beef
1 Medium sized potato, peeled and diced very fine
1 t. salt
½ t. pepper
1 C. Panko or dry bread crumbs
1 Egg, whipped
¾ C. onion, chopped

Mix everything together. Get your hands right in there and mix, mix, mix. Form into balls about the size of walnuts. Place on a cookie sheet which onto which you have placed a foil protector. Bake in a 350° oven for about ¾ of an hour. I used to serve these delicious creatures with beans, apple sauce, brown bread and butter.

LUCILLE MAGILL'S SYRIAN MEAT BALLS

May use grape leaves or cabbage. If using cabbage, cut out center of head. Clean grape leaves and cabbage. Put in boiling water for about 5 minutes.

1 lb. ground lamb
1 cup rice to 1 lb. lamb

Wash rice thoroughly and mix with meat. Put in ¼ t. pepper, pinch of cinnamon. Add salt to your liking. Mix the ingredients with the lamb and rice. Take a small amount of meat and rice mixture and put on a leaf and roll the leaf once around the mixture. Cook with either tomato juice or sliced tomatoes and add more salt when cooking. Cook until tender.

SWEDISH PORK SAUSAGES

Another of Elaine Selander's contributions. Elaine and I had a lovely week-end one summer a few years back. We made these sausages together, talked about when she and my mother were young women in Whitehall, Michigan and reminisced about a lot of happenings around the little town on White Lake where I grew up. She was very close to 90 then and left us not too many years later.

1 Lb. pork fat (without meat)
2 Lb. lean ground pork
1 Lb ground beef
  [Have your butcher run ½ of the pork fat + 2 lbs. lean ground pork and 1 lb. gr. beef through the grinder 3 times].
1 Lb. potatoes, peeled and cooked 12 minutes (cool overnight then mash)
½ C. potato flour
5 t. salt
1 t. ginger
1 ½ t. coarsely ground pepper
1 t. coarsely ground allspice
½ t. cloves
½ t. salt peter
5 C. boiled, cold milk or strong pork stock or canned undiluted consommé
6 Yards straight or round casings –about 2 inches wide into which the ingredients which you have mixed well together have been stuffed (I invested in a sausage maker.)

Curing: Rub on sausages- 4 T. salt, 2 T. sugar, 1 t. salt peter

Cook: Simmer with 1 bay leaf, 10 pepper corns or allspice and ½ t. salt.

Those Swedes really knew how to cook!

POTATO SAUSAGE-

An old family recipe of Swedish decent that must be followed exactly!

6 Lb. beef (not too lean)
5 Lb. potatoes (No, 10 can Irish whole potatoes with liquid drained)
4 ½ Lb. pork (not too lean)
2 Large onions chopped
2 ½ oz. of salt (or 5 T.)
½ Oz. black pepper (or 1 Tablespoon)

Cut beef and pork into medium sized chunks. (It should not be too lean because the fat in it soaks up the potato starch). Leave potatoes whole. Put these ingredients in a large pan. Then add seasonings and mix. Add onions and mix. Then grind everything at once. Stuff in casings or make into patties or use as a meat loaf. The Swede who shared this recipe says that he puts one sausage in a skillet with water to cover, brings it to a boil and then turns the heat to a simmer and covers it. The sausage will be cooked after 20 minutes of simmering. You can also freeze your makings

HAMBURGERS WITH ALMONDS

2 pounds ground chuck
2 teaspoons fines herbs (Herbs de Provence will be fine)
1 5 1/2-ounce package almonds, slivered or chopped lengthwise
1 t. MSG (leave out if allergic)
Salt and pepper to taste

Sprinkle almonds on a cookie sheet and toast in a preheated over to crisp them. Be careful not to let them burn. Mix ground chuck, slivered almonds, fines herbes, and seasonings together. Don't handle the meat too much. Form into patties. Pan grill or cook in a skillet with a little oil and butter as you would any other burger. Serve on a toasted, buttered burger bun. Do not add any of the usual condiments. They are wonderful just as they are. Serves 8

FILLED HAMBURGERS OR INSIDEOUT BURGERS FROM THE '60s OF THE 20TH CENTURY

Use ground round, ground chuck or a mixture

Take 2 smaller than regular size patties. Flatten between pieces of wax paper. Spread a little mustard on the bottom patty and catsup if you like. Then put over that mixture, 1 teaspoon of chopped fresh onion, 1 teaspoon pickled relish and 1 tablespoon grated sharp Cheddar (or cheese if your choice). Leave a little room on the outer edges of the hamburger. Place top patty over bottom and press outer edges together. Season with salt, pepper and MSG (unless allergic to it).

Fry, grill or broil – but only turn once and carefully so that the filling stays in the hamburger.
Serve with or without a bun.
Serves 4 to 6 (using two pounds of meat)

AUNTIE GREET AND COUSIN MARGO'S PORK OR BEEF BBQ

2 lbs. pork or beef roast – sprinkle meat with a little onion, celery and garlic salt. Chop one large onion and put in roasting pan with 2 cups of water. Cook meat at 325° for several hours. Note: Cook until you can take a couple of forks and pull the meat apart (shredded).

Sauce: Drain ½ cup of stock from roasting pan and put in a separate pan adding the following:

1 C. tomato juice	1/8 t. pepper
¼ C. vinegar	2 T. Worcestershire
½ C. stock from meat	1 t. salt
2 T. brown sugar	¼ C. sugar

Cook sauce in pan until it begins to thicken. Pour over shredded beef or pork, mix and serve on buns.

SPOONBURGERS

The Brey boys, Hal and Jarl, were raised on this sloppy-jo recipe I got from a Delta Gamma alumna cookbook. Freeze some of it for small servings, serve it to a large crowd or get a little snazzy and serve it from a chafing dish onto slider buns.

Brown 5 pounds hamburger, pour off almost, but not all, grease. Add the following:

5 T. sugar   3 T. Worcestershire sauce
5 T. tarragon vinegar   3 C. catsup
5 T. dry mustard   2 Medium size cans of mushrooms
Simmer for ½ hour uncovered and ½ hour covered. Serves 15

AUNT EVA'S BARBEQUED BEEF

She wasn't really my aunt, but I have always called her so. She was a close friend of Auntie Greet and cooked in the same circle of excellence as she. Owning a summer hotel was one of her accomplishments and making the best lemon meringue pie was just another. Here is her recipe for barbequed beef:

1 ½ lbs. ground beef
1 T. fat

Cook together in a sauce:
        1 T. lemon juice
        2 T. vinegar
        ¼ C. water
        1 ¼ C. catsup
        1 t. dry mustard
        1 ½ t. salt
        2 T. brown sugar
        1 T. onion, cut fine
        1 C. celery, cut fine
Cook beef in a large frying pan, stirring frequently. Add to the sauce. Heat thoroughly. Serve on buns.

U.S. 31 BAR-B-Q

If you are old enough to remember the infamous U.S. 31 Bar-B-Q in Muskegon, Michigan, you are blessed. If I had had a bad day at work, I would drive from Grand Rapids to Muskegon to indulge myself in their specialty, Pork Bar-B-Qs, and think that I had died and gone to heaven. I finally shared my secret with best buddies, Dan Switek and Roxanne Gerds who would make the trek with me. Apparently people from across the country have had them wrapped and shipped in dry ice. Yes, they are that good, although my eldest son, Hal, prefers the south western version with a different sauce. Nevertheless I am offering these to you. You can freeze the sauce and if you really enjoy ham or beef, spoon some on those.

1 ¼ Lb. cabbage
¼ Lb. onions

Grind these together with a hand grinder or invest in a food processor.

1 C. sweet pickle relish
½ C. catsup
¼ C. mustard
¼ C. vinegar (use a light white wine vinegar)
½ to ¾ C. of white sugar (your taster will tell you)
1/8 of a 5.8 Oz. bottle of horseradish
¼ Small jar of pimento cut small

Bring to a simmer to heat thoroughly, stir once in a while. Heat separately from the meat and spread over pork (or ham or beef) which has been placed on a bun. It's pretty messy to eat, but that's half the fun.

SWANKY FRANKS

One spring break when I was visiting my brother, Mack, in Atlanta, we ventured to the glorious home of a former ballet dancer and model who turned interior designer. Don't remember her name, but she had a full time maid and a daughter who danced with a New York ballet company. My brother had dated the daughter, Monica. Anyway the maid made a quick lunch for us and served it on china, with crystal water glasses and I was impressed thinking how wonderful humble food can be when dressed up.

1 hot dog (I suppose that you could also use a cooked bratworst)
Left over mashed potatoes
Grated cheese of your choice
Bacon

Make a horizontal slit in the hot dog but try not do cut completely through. Fill the opening with mashed potatoes and sprinkle with grated cheese. Wrap bacon around the filled hot dog and place in a 400 degree oven until cheese melts and bacon is cooked. Serve with a plate of fresh tomatoes. Yummo!

SHRIMP SALAD SANDWICH

I cracked this recipe thirty years ago after I became addicted to it in one of the Grand Rapids restaurants which no longer exists. I kept tasting and tasting and finally I had it. . . . . .and I share my findings.

2 C. shrimp, cut up
½ C. celery, finely sliced
¾ C. coconut
¼ C. sour cream
Enough good mayo to moisten the above first 3 ingredients.

Throw everything into a medium sized bowl. Then mix and mix. Toast your choice of bread, butter 3- slices per sandwich, slather the mixture on each of two slices and stack. Put some leaf lettuce on each layer to give color, perhaps secure a bread and butter pickle to the top and serve with chips and a small plain fruit salad.

PRESSED CUBANO WITH BACON

There was a café in Plainwell, Michigan which was a favorite of mine. Its name was Aries. I would eat alone, drag friends from Grand Rapids or Kalamazoo, or meet people at this wonderful restaurant which served anything divine. Their desserts were renowned! It no longer exists, more's the pity. Here is a wonderful Cuban sandwich they served which is great for lunch or supper as well.

Garlic oil gives these sandwiches a crisp, flavorful crust. Hawaiian rolls provide a slightly sweet contrast to the salty ham, pickles and mustard or be creative if you can't find these. To make this easy supper even quicker to prepare, use pre-cooked bacon, if you wish . Serve with banana peppers.

1 t. extra virgin olive oil
1 Garlic clove, minced
4 (3 oz.) Hawaiian rolls, sliced in half horizontally
2 T. yellow mustard
8 (1/2 oz.) slices Swiss cheese, divided
4 Bacon slices, cooked and halved
12 Dill pickle slices
2 t. minced fresh cilantro
6 oz. thinly sliced ham
2 oz. thinly sliced deli roasted turkey breasts

After filling the rolls, grill them in a heavy skillet, using an aluminum covered brick to weigh it down and watch carefully. Use a large spatula to flip it. A most tasty fare.

SURPRISE PARTY SANDWICH LOAF

The surprise is the sour cream meringue that frosts the loaf, but there's delectability in every bite with three cheese based fillings inside. Adding glamour to the party table, this sandwich loaf makes a light but satisfying main course for a luncheon, shower or as a light main course with dinner. I served this with fruit salad, vegetable gelatin mold and relishes . . . .and that was in the 1960s when two little Brey boys were circling my knees.

10-12 SERVINGS

1 Loaf (1 ¼ Lb.) unsliced sandwich bread
½ C. (1 stick) butter, softened
1 Recipe Egg-Cheese filling
1 Recipe Tuna-Cheese filling
2 Medium tomatoes, sliced
1 Recipe Olive-Cheese filling
2 Medium tomatoes, sliced
1 Recipe Olive-Cheese filling
1 Recipe Sour Cream "meringue"
Tomato wedges, stuffed olives and water cress for garnish

Remove crusts from bread; cut loaf into 4 lengthwise slices; spread each cut slice with butter. Place bottom slice, buttered side up, on a baking sheet and spread with Egg-Cheese filling. Cover with second slice of bread and spread with Tuna -Cheese filling; top with tomato slices. Cover with third slice of bread and spread with Olive-Cheese filling. Top with fourth slice of bread. Loaf may be assembled in advance, wrapped in waxed paper and refrigerated. Just before serving prepare Sour Cream "meringue" and frost top and sides of loaf. Garnish platter with tomato wedges, stuffed olives and water cress.

Egg – Cheese Filling

4 Hard-cooked eggs
½ C. cottage or ricotta cheese
3 T. sweet pickle relish
½ t. salt
Chop eggs, mix thoroughly with cheese, pickle relish and salt.

Tuna-Cheese Filling

1-7 oz. can of tuna fish (packed in water), drained
1- 3 oz. package cream cheese
2 T. milk
1 T. prepared mustard
¼ C. chopped peanuts
   Mix together tuna fish, cream cheese, milk and mustard until well blended; stir in peanuts.

Olive-Cheese Filling

1½ C. shredded Cheddar cheese
½ C. dairy sour cream
¼ C. chopped ripe olives
¼ t. chili powder
   Mix together Cheddar cheese and sour cream, blend in olives and chili powder.

I have also found two other lovely fillings if you want to change them around.

Lobster Salad Filling

Cut one cup cooked and drained lobster into small pieces; mix with 1 t. lemon juice, l t. minced onion, ½ C. diced celery, ½ C. mayo, salt and paprika to taste and mix well.

Chicken Salad Filling

Chop 5 Oz. cooked, boned chicken (canned may be used) and mix with ¼ cup chopped toasted almonds, ½ C. minced celery 1 T. lemon juice and 1 t. grated onion, ½ C. mayo., salt and pepper to taste and mix well

Sour Cream "Meringue"

½ t. salt
2 pkg. softened cream cheese (8 oz. each)
1 C. dairy sour cream

Beat the softened cream cheese and salt together, gently fold in sour cream until blended. Frost sides and top, adding grape tomatoes, olives and chives for garnish.

BLOODY MARY FLANK STEAK

1 C. V-8 juice
½ C. vodka
1 t. sea salt
1 t. freshly ground black pepper
1 t. hot sauce
1 T. lemon juice
1 T. Worcestershire sauce
½ T. crushed garlic
1 t. onion powder
1 t. celery seed
1 T. prepared horseradish
4 T. olive oil
1 Lb. flank steak

Thoroughly mix all the ingredients except for the flank steak in a 1-gallon zip lock bag. Add the flank steak. Marinate in the refrigerator for at least 8 and up to 24 hours.

Preheat the grill to high or heat a skillet over high heat. Remove the flank steak from the marinade and wipe the excess liquid off the paper towels. Grill or pan sear both sides, then lower the heat to medium and cook to medium rare.

Let the flank steak rest, covered, with a clean towel for 5-10 minutes. Cut on the bias against the grain and serve.

JIMMY'S JEWISH HOLIDAY BRISKET

Recipe from Florence Obstfeld- My best Oregon buddy. Jimmy is her son.

4 lb. Brisket
2 Large onions
2 Stalks celery
2 Bay leaves
1 Bottle Chili sauce
¼ C. water
4 Cloves garlic
¼ C. brown sugar
1/3 C. Dijon mustard
1/3 C. red wine vinegar
3 T. molasses
¼ C. soy sauce

Oven at 325 degrees for 4 hours.

Put sliced onions, celery and bay leaves on top of meat. Mix remaining sauce ingredients and pour over meat. Bake as directed. When cooked take meat out of pan and pour sauce in bowl. Chill both the sauce and meat (sliced). Next day pour sauce over beef after skimming off fat. Warm up meat.

TLC: Save bones and leftovers in a special place in the freezer and combine later for a great soup. Always add one fresh vegetable for a lively taste

FOOLPROOF STANDING RIB ROAST

I love the recipes from the south. They are scrumptious and if you notice are filled with BUTTER— yup, butter. I make them anyway just once in a awhile. Julia used a lot of butter which made her recipes divine; so there. This recipe is from Paula Deen, a wonderfully gracious southern lady who had a cooking show and inspired a lot of people. I have used it and used it when I could afford a standing rib. They go on sale at Christmas time so remember that. This is easy and turns out beautifully if you follow the directions to the tee.

5 lb. standing rib roast

Rub with seasoning (seasoning the roast using a mixture of 1 C. salt, ¼ C. garlic powder, ¼ C. black pepper. Mix well and store in a good container) – no you do not use the entire amount on the rib roast – it is used as a basic seasoning for lots of other things as well

Follow this method for a rib roast that is lusciously browned on the outside and rare on the inside - - -- - REGARDLESS OF SIZE. Allow roast to stand at room temperature for at least 1 hour. If roast is frozen, thaw completely in the refrigerator and then bring to room temperature. Preheat oven to 375 degrees, Rub roast with Seasoning; place roast on rack in pan---rib side down, fatty side up. Roast for 1 hour. Turn oven off. Leave roast in oven BUT DO NOT OPEN OVEN DOOR. Thirty to 40 minutes before serving time, turn oven back on to 375 degrees to reheat roast. Important: Do not remove roast or open oven door from time roast is put in until ready to serve.

CALIFORNIA SAUERBRATEN

I got this recipe from Parade Magazine (Sunday insert of the 1970's) and it is very good, I used it for years. The recipe is so old that the newsprint is yellow with age and it is missing the amount of red wine. I guessed.

4 C. red wine
1 ½ C. wine vinegar
1 C. water
3 T. light brown sugar
1 C. dried prunes
8 Small onions, halved
1 t. whole black pepper
¼ t, powdered bay leaves
8 Whole allspice
2-Inch stick cinnamon
8 Whole cloves
1 t. salt
4 Lb. boned and rolled beef chuck
3 T. vegetable oil

Combine first 12 ingredients, pour over meat. Marinate in refrigerator 24 to 48 hours, turning several times. Remove meat; pat dry. Remove prunes; set aside. Brown meat slowly on all sides in vegetable oil. Pour off any remaining oil. Add marinade. Cover; simmer 2 ½ to 3 hours or until meat is tender. Remove meat; keep warm. Pit prunes; add to meat stock, simmer 10 minutes. Remove prunes. Strain stock; measure; thicken with flour mixed smooth with an equal amount of cold water, using 1 to 2 tablespoons per cup of cold water, using 1 or 2 tablespoons per cup of stock according to thickness desired. Garnish meat with prunes. Serve gravy separately.

SAUERBRATEN RECIPE FROM GERMANY

The Brey boys Christmas Treat. The secret of this recipe is to let the roast marinate for 3 full days. This recipe comes directly from Germany. This classic, but easy, recipe requires advanced planning and time (3 days!), but it has a flavor and aroma that is incredible.

Marinade Ingredients:
1 C. dry red wine
1 C. red wine vinegar
2 C. cold water
1 Medium onion, thinly sliced
1 T. black peppercorns, coarsely crushed
1 T. juniper berries, coarsely crushed
2 Bay leaves
1 t. salt
2 – 3 T. sauerbraten Spice

Roasting/Sauce Ingredients:

4 pounds boneless beef roast, preferable bottom round
3 T. butter
2 T. flour
½ C. Water
¾ C. gingersnap cookies, crumbled
2 ½ C. onions, diced
2 ½ C. carrots, diced
1 ¼ C. celery, diced

Yields 6-8 servings

Combine all marinade ingredients, except the roast itself, in 2-3 quart sauce pan. Bring to boil over high heat. Remove from heat and allow to cool to room temperature.

(Continued on next page)

Place the beef in a deep, non-reactive (glass or ceramic) bowl or pot just large enough to hold it. Pour marinade over beef. The marinade should be at least halfway up the sides of the roast. If necessary add more wine. Cover tightly with foil or plastic wrap and refrigerate for 2 – 3 days, turning the meat in the marinade at least twice each day.

Remove meat from marinade and pat completely dry with paper towels. Strain the marinade through a fine sieve and reserve the liquid. Discard spices and onions.

Transfer the roast to a heated platter and cover with foil to keep warm while sauce is made.

Pour the liquid left in the pot into a large measuring cup and skim fat from surface. You will need at least 2 ½ cups for the sauce. If additional liquid is needed, add some of the reserved marinade.

Combine the liquid and the gingersnap crumbs in a saucepan and cook over moderate heat, stirring frequently for approx. 10 minutes, allowing the cookie crumbs to dissolve completely and thicken the sauce to the desired consistency. Depending upon the amount of liquid, you may need to add additional cookie crumbs.

Strain the sauce through a fine sieve, pressing down hard with a wooden spoon to force as much of the vegetables and crumbs through as possible. Return the sauce to the pan, adjust seasoning and allow it to simmer over low heat until ready to serve.

Slice the roast, pour some sauce over slices on platter and pass remaining sauce separately.

Helpful Hints: Traditionally, sauerbraten is served with dumplings, boiled potatoes, spaetzle, and red cabbage. (I usually serve egg noodles, cold red cabbage as a salad, chunky applesauce and Hot German potato salad – this works for me).

Don't hesitate to adjust the amount of gingersnap cookies to give the sauce your preferred consistency. The flavorful gingersnap cookies are used as the thickener, not flour, so you don't run the risk of having a pasty sauce.

JKM'S GERMAN ROAST FOR TWO BREY BOYS – AN ODE

This was a favorite of my sons (I told them it was a German roast and they bought it). It is a very delicious, very hearty dish for colder weather fare starting around October and ending in April.

I used a three pound boneless chuck roast for my small family.

Place it in a slow cooker on low or very low oven.
Throw a small can of mushrooms on top.
Then a can of garlic mushroom soup, undiluted.
On the top I planted an envelope of onion soup mix.

Let this beauty go for the day. I served it with egg noodles, using the sauce for gravy and made a Waldorf salad (I always use dates instead of raisins in this along with walnuts, apples and celery – just seems to go with this dish.

GERMAN ROULADEN

(Meat rolls filled with bacon, onions and dill pickles)

Eldest son, Hal, discovered this at a bistro in Rockford, Michigan which was run by a retired doctor who had always wanted to own café and be the chef. Well, he did and was! Hal returned after taking his homecoming date out and related what they had chosen to eat. I had never heard of rouladen, but I listened carefully as he explained the taste, and its presentation. I have made it for the Brey boys every Christmas since.

At Christmas time, I would honor part of my sons' ethnic background and make a killer German dinner which took me hours to put together though they enjoyed every minute of every bite. Perched at the top of their dinner plates was an orange with a lighted tapered candle stuffed into it. This was accompanied by German bread and rolls, Usinger bratwurst ordered from Wisconsin (although the Amish make wonderful brats if you are anywhere near a community of them), rouladen, sauerbraten with a gravy sauce to pour over the egg noodles, German potato salad, chilled sweet and sour red cabbage, baked beans and apple pie. I will make sure that the recipes are included in this book. My mouth waters as I type. The table was always special and we truly gave thanks for our blessings.

Serves 6

1 ½ Lb. of flank steak (6 pieces– have the butcher cut them for you and run them two or three times through the tenderizing machine.

Salt and pepper to taste

Stone ground mustard to taste

½ Lb. thick sliced bacon   2 Large onions, diced

1 16 oz. jar of dill (not kosher) pickles (either the wedged slices or the flat ones)

2 T. of butter   2 ½ C. water   2 Cubes of beef bouillon

1. Generously spread one of each filet with salt and pepper and mustard to taste. Place bacon, onions and pickle slices on each filet and form into a roll. Use string or toothpicks to hold the roll together.

2. Heat a skillet over medium heat and melt butter. Place the rolls in the butter and sauté until browned. Place the browned rouladen in a Dutch oven and pour in the water with the bouillon. Set in a 350 degree oven for an hour or until tender.

GERMAN-STYLE POT ROAST

Here is another recipe for a sauerbraten style roast that is quite good and can be done in a slow cooker. I have made it several times; enjoyed it, sent it to sick friends and passed the recipe on. . . . . .and it is ever so easy.

4-5 Lbs, boneless chuck or bottom round roast

¾ C. cider vinegar
¼ C. ketchup
½ C. chopped onion
1 t. finely chopped garlic

2 14-Oz cans beef broth
12 Ginger snap cookies
2 8-Oz envelopes brown gravy mix

Combine all ingredients, except the meat, in a crock-pot. Stir well. Add the meat and stir well to coat. Cover and cook on low for 10 hours or on high for 5 hours. Makes 8-10 servings. I serve this with butter noodles. German food is not for the dieter!!!

BOEF BOURGUIGNON

Don't let the title scare you, it's simply beef stew, wonderful beef stew.
This is the recipe that was the impetus as well as cincher for Julia Child's success with her *Mastering the Art of French Cooking* book. Takes a good while to make, but is worth every minute of your labor. Bon Appetit! . . . and thanks Ina.

– serves 6.

1 T. good olive oil
8 oz. dry cured center cut applewood smoked bacon, diced
2 ½ lbs. chuck beef cut into 1 inch cubes
Kosher salt
Freshly ground black pepper
1 Lb. carrots, sliced diagonally into 1 inch chunks
2 Yellow onions, sliced
2 t. chopped garlic (2 cloves)
½ C. Cognac
1 (750 ml) Bottle of good dry red wine
1 Can (2 cups) beef broth

(Continued on next page)

1 T. tomato paste
1 t. fresh thyme leaves (1/2 t. dried)
4 T. unsalted butter at room temperature, divided
3 T all-purpose flour
1 Lb. frozen whole onions (small ones in freezer case)
1 Lb. fresh mushrooms, stems discarded, caps thickly sliced

For Serving: Country bread or Sour Dough, toasted or grilled and rubbed with garlic clove and ½ C. chopped fresh parsley, optional

Heat the olive oil in a large Dutch oven. Add the bacon and cook over medium heat for 10 minutes, stirring occasionally until the bacon is lightly browned. Remove the bacon with a slotted spoon to a large plate.

Dry the beef cubes with paper towels and then sprinkle them with salt and pepper. In batches in single layers, sear the beef in the hot oil for 3 to 5 minutes turning to brown on all sides. Remove the seared cubes to the plate with the bacon and continue searing until all the beef is browned. Set aside.

Toss the carrots, and onions, 1 tablespoon of salt and 2 teaspoons of pepper in the fat for 10 to 15 minutes, stirring occasionally, until the onions are lightly browned. Add the garlic and cook for 1 more minute. Add the Cognac, stand back and ignite with a match to burn off the alcohol. Put the meat and bacon back into the pot with juices. Add the bottle of wine plus enough beef broth to almost cover the meat. Add the tomato paste and thyme. Bring to a simmer, cover the pot with a tight-fitting lid and place it in the oven(350) for about 1 ¼ hours or until the meat and vegetables are very tender when pierced with a fork.

Combine 2 tablespoons of butter and the flour with a fork and stir into the stew. Add frozen onions. Saute the mushrooms in 2 tablespoons of butter for 10 minutes until lightly browned and then add to the stew. Bring the stew to a boil on top of the stove, then lower the heat and simmer for 15 minutes. Season to taste.

To serve, toast the bread in the toaster or oven. Rub each slice on 1 side with a cut clove of garlic. For each serving. Spoon the stew over a slice of bread and sprinkle with parsley.

SPAGHETTI PIE

1 ½ Lb. ground beef
1 Medium onion, chopped
1 Stalk celery, chopped
1 – 16 oz. can tomatoes, chopped
1 – 6 oz. can tomato paste
Salt, pepper and sugar to taste
6 – 8 oz. spaghetti (depending on size of group)
¼ C. butter, melted
1/3 C. grated parmesan cheese
2 Eggs, beaten
1 C. cottage cheese
1 ½ C. (6 oz.) shredded mozzarella cheese

Brown meat and drain. Add onion and celery. Cook until tender. Stir in tomatoes and tomato paste. Season to taste with salt, pepper and sugar. Mix well. Simmer 20 minutes.

Cook spaghetti and drain. Combine with butter, parmesan cheese and eggs. Mix well. Line a greased 9x13 pan with spaghetti. Spoon cottage cheese over spaghetti. Top with mozzarella and then meat sauce.
Bake 45 minutes at 325.

AVOCADO - OLE

6 Tostada shells
1 Can (16 oz.) refried beans
½ C. finely chopped onion
2 T. flour
¾ C. red taco sauce
½ t. garlic powder

½ C. grated longhorn cheese
1 Tomato in wedges
1 C. sour cream
1 ripe avocado, peeled, seeded and sliced
½ Head lettuce, shredded

Brown ground beef. Add onion; cook until transparent. Add flour, taco sauce, garlic powder. Heat thoroughly. Set aside

Layer tostada: Start with tostada shell, a generous helping of heated refried beans, meat mixture, lettuce, cheese. Place dollop of sour cream on side. Arrange wedges of tomato along the edge and slices of avocado on top of tostada. Garnish with sour cream. 6 servings,

PATTI VOLKEL'S CABBAGE ROLLS

1 Lb. ground beef
1 Small chopped onion
½ C. rice, uncooked
2 8-Oz. cans tomato sauce

Salt and pepper to taste
1 Head Cabbage
2 Eggs
2 Cans (1 lb. 13 oz.) tomatoes

Mix together the first 5 ingredients well. Use 12 leaves cabbage which you will want to soak in boiling water until soft enough to roll. Put a mound of mixture in a leaf and roll; fasten with toothpick.

Spread Dutch oven with cabbage leaves and place rolls, seam side down. Pour Tomatoes and tomato sauce over them.

For the sauce on top: 1 large onion, chopped; Juice of 2 lemons and pour on top. Sprinkle with brown sugar to taste also add a little more salt and pepper to taste.

Boil on top of stove to get the ingredients going and then bake 1 hour, covered and 1 hour uncovered in a 375 degree oven.

2 LAYER MEAT SURPRISE
AND BARRY SMITH'S BONANZA

Joanna Braun gave me this recipe in the early 1960's. She did not consider herself a good cook; she was an artist who had taught elementary school and painted. I really liked this recipe. . . .It was easy and tasted like country fare and rang well at church potlucks. I also once had a trainer whose name was Barry Smith and he threw a jar of spaghetti sauce on the meat mixture instead of mushroom soup and covered the whole thing with corn muffin mix after mixing that up.

Saute in a couple of T. butter till limp:
> ½ C. thinly sliced celery
> 1 Large chopped onion

Add: 1 Lb. ground beef and break up the mixture
> while incorporating the above 2
Add: 1 ½ T. Worcestershire sauce and blend
Add: 1 Can cream of mushroom soup and blend

Mix up a package of instant corn bread/muffins. Make sure that the meat mixture is still hot when you place it in a casserole pan. Immediately top the mixture with the corn muffin /bread mixture you have prepared and pop in a 350° oven for 20 to 30 minutes or until golden brown. Spoon out and serve with a green salad.

DEEP DISH TATER TOT/ MEAT CASSAROLE

In deep casserole dish, put a 1" layer of uncooked meat. Top with slices of onion and layer of tater tots. Season each layer of meat , continue to alternate layers until about 1" from top of dish. Pour 2 cans of mushroom soup and 1 cup of milk over completed dish. Bake 1 -2 hours in slow (300 degrees) oven. May not need entire pkg. of tater tots.

EASY TACO PIE

(serves 6)

1 Lb. ground beef	1 C. milk
1 Medium onion, chopped (1/2 cup)	2 Eggs
1 Envelope of taco seasoning mix	¾ C. shredded Monterey Jack or Cheddar
1 Can chopped green chilies, drained	Salsa, if desired
½ C. Bisquick	Sour Cream, if desired

Heat oven to 400 degrees. Grease pie plate. 9 x 1 1/4 inches. Cook beef and onions in 10 inch skillet over medium heat. Stirring occasionally until beef is brown, drain. Stir in mix (dry). Spread in pie place. Add cheese and top with chilies. Blend the Bisquick, milk and eggs and spread over mixture. Stick in the oven for 30 minutes. Check to see if the top is golden and done.

THAT CASSEROLE

1 ½ Lb. ground beef	8 oz. sour cream
Garlic salt to taste	6 Green onions, minced
1 (15 ounce) Tomato sauce	1 T. minced green pepper
6 oz. thin egg noodles	1 C. grated cheese or cottage cheese
3 oz. cream cheese	

Saute ground beef. Add garlic salt and tomato sauce. Simmer about 10 minutes. Cook noodles as directed on package. Drain. Mix together cream cheese, sour cream, and green onions. Layer ingredients in casserole, beginning with noodles, meat sauce, and sour cream mixture, ending with grated cheese on top. Cover and bake 1 hour at 350 degrees. Serves 4 . . . . .unless they are teenagers!

TLC: As you cook, cook, cook - - -taste, taste, taste and correct

JARL BREY'S SPAGETE

The Michigan winter storm of 1978 was horrendous; I got stranded at school in a complete whiteout while my 15 year old son was home. I had to stay with my secretary while Jarl called every 15 minutes to ask about making spaghetti. This is his own concoction and spelling and I just love it.

8 oz. tomato sauce
12 oz. tomato paste
16 oz. stewed tomatoes
Salt and pepper to taste
Parmesan cheese

1 chopped onion
1 lb. ground beef
1 Shake of red pepper
1 T. white wine
Packet of spaghetti sauce mix and seasoning
(probably a couple of shakes of oregano, rosemary, basil—who knows)

Mix everything and let simmer for a long time. Eventually pour over pasta.

DAGO MARGE'S SPAGHETTI SAUCE

My father, Charles Margrave (known as Chuck), managed Saginaw's Moonlight Gardens in his late 20s and early 30s. He also was a drummer for a band that traveled through the (then 48) United States. He settled in Saginaw, Michigan where he met and married my mother, Dorothy. Though mother was a very simple cook, one of the things she excelled at was Dago Marge's spaghetti recipe from Italy. Dago Marge, as she was called, would make this daily for my dad's menu fare at the night club. When I was probably in my first year of high school and then living in Whitehall, Michigan, I finally got to meet her and taste her wonderful sauce. She put a great big white napkin around my neck which I of course messed up with sauce as I gobbled this delight.

3 Cans tomato paste
3 Cans water
1 Onion, chopped
Olive oil
1 Lb. ground beef

1 Can mushrooms
Salt and pepper
2 Cloves of garlic, chopped fine
1 t. Oregano

Cover bottom of pan with olive oil, add ground beef, salt, pepper, garlic, onion, mushrooms and simmer, stirring occasionally. Add tomato paste and water and stir to incorporate. TASTE, then add more seasoning if needed. Cover and let sauce simmer on very low for 3 hours.

REAL SPAGHETTI SAUCE

1 ½ - 2 C. Celery chopped
1 Med. sized red onion, chopped
2 Cloves of garlic, finely chopped
2 C. chopped fresh parsley
1 Green pepper, chopped
3 or 4 Fresh tomatoes peeled or
2 Cans of tomatoes or use both
1 Large can or equal fresh mushroom,
   cooked
1 Pkg. Lawrey's spaghetti sauce
2 Cans tomato paste
6 C. of water
2 t. dry mustard

2 t. Italian seasoning
1 t. garlic salt
1 t. salt
1 t. ground pepper
½ t. nutmeg
½ t. sage
1 t. fennel seeds
2 T. olive oil
¼ C. sugar
1 – 1 ½ C. grated parmesan
           or Romano cheese
Dash of bitters
1 – ½ C. red wine

Make meat balls and brown in oil and add to the sauce (you can also use the frozen ones from the freezer dept. which are excellent) or you may use browned ground beef.

Cook sauce several hours – preferably all day (why not use a crock pot on low). When adding wine, add only ¼ cup at one time. As if there aren't enough ingredients, add Pygmalion nuts and Italian hot sausage to this sauce also, but sparingly.   Serves 8-19

MACARONI AND CHEESE

All of my grandchildren: Elyse, Charlie, Mackenzie and Parker grew up on mac n' cheese dinners out of the Kraft box and loved them. No offense, Ms. Kraft, but I like my own recipe even better! And so . . . . :

2 C. uncooked macaroni
2 Qt. water
2 t. salt
1/3 C. butter
1/3 C. flour
Salt and pepper to taste
2/3 C. cream or ½ and ½ or rich milk
2 C. grated cheeses: try ½ C. of gruyere, ½ C. cheddar, ½ C. Swiss, and perhaps a small tube of goat cheese with garlic/chive flavoring and just to add a little more, ½ C. of Munster cheese, grated. Yes I Know!
1/8 t. paprika
Few grains of cayenne
Throw a few sprinkles of nutmeg in
1 C. sour cream

Cook the macaroni in the water with the salt for 10 to 12 minutes and drain. Melt butter in a saucepan. Add flour, salt and pepper, paprika, cayenne and nutmeg, stirring constantly. Add milk and cheese until mixture begins to thicken. Add sour cream and macaroni. Continue cooking for several minutes over low heat, letting the flavors impart.

CHEESEMONGER'S MAC AND CHEESE

Another winner for Mac –n- Cheese

Suzi Mittlesteadt sent this recipe to me and I shared it at a summer gathering. The Guests raved and asked for the recipe.

1 ½ C. coarsely grated Gruyere cheese (Suzi's favorite cheese)
1 ½ C. coarsely grated sharp cheddar cheese (about 6 oz.)
1 ½ C. diced rindless Brie (cut from 1 pound wedge)
5 Tablespoons butter, divided
¼ C. all purpose flour
2 t. chopped fresh thyme leaves
¾ (scant) t. nutmeg
4 C. whole milk
1 ¾ C. fresh breadcrumbs made from crustless French bread
1 Lb. penne pasta (or that of your choice)
8 t. whipping cream (if making 1 day ahead)

Mix all cheeses. Set aside 1 cup for topping, cover and chill. Melt 4 tablespoons butter in large saucepan over medium heat. Add flour and stir until mixture turns golden brown, about 4 minutes. Add thyme and nutmeg. Gradually whisk in milk. Simmer until thickened and smooth, stirring often, about 4 minutes,. Add cheeses from large bowl. Stir until melted and smooth.

Melt 1 tablespoon butter I heavy large skillet over medium-high heat. Add breadcrumbs; toss. Stir until golden, about 2 minutes. Transfer to plate. Pre-heat oven to 375 degrees. Cook pasta in boiling water until tender but firm to bite. Drain. Transfer to large bowl. Pour cheese sauce over; toss. Divide among eight 1 ¼ -cup custard cups.. Sprinkle with 1 cup cheese. Place cups on rimmed baking sheet.

Can be made 1 day ahead.

MARY LOU GREEN'S LASAGNA

8 oz. Pkg. lasagna noodles, *cooked*
Meat sauce: 1 lb. ground beef
              1 ½ t. garlic salt
              1 ½ t. Lawry's salt
              ½ lemon pepper
              ½ Green pepper, chopped
              1 T. basil
              ½ t. onion powder
              ½ t. Italian seasoning
              2 C. stewed tomatoes
              1 Small can tomato paste

Brown meat and mix with above ingredients; simmer ½ hr. or longer

Cheese filling: 2 C. small curd cottage cheese
              2 T. flat leaf parsley
              2 eggs. beaten slightly
              ½ C. grated Ragu cheese
Combine the above ingrediants.
Add: 1 lb. Mozzarella cheese, shredded.

Place some noodles int 14 x 10 x 3 inch pan, then cheese filling, then meat filling, then the mozzarella. Repeat layers, trying to end up with the meat layer on top. Bake at 350° for ½ hour or more. Give the dish a 10-minute rest before serving.

DUCKLING A L'ORANGE

You can do this one, just follow the directions and you will wow yourself!
Nice to serve with white rice combined with sautéed sliced mushrooms.

5 Lb. ready-to-cook duckling (If frozen, completely thaw)
1 t. salt
1 Large onion, peeled
1 Clove garlic, chopped

3 Whole black peppers
2 Unpeeled oranges, quartered
½ C. Burgundy

Orange Sauce

3 T. butter
Liver from duckling
2 T. grated orange peel
3/4 t. chopped garlic
2 T. flour
2 t. catsup
1 Chicken-bouillon cube
1 ¼ C. broth from giblets

Dash pepper
3 T. brandy
1/3 C. Burgundy
¼ C. orange marmalade
¼ C. Orange juice
1 C. orange sections
½ C. orange marmalade

1. Remove giblets and neck from duckling and reserve. Wash duckling under running water; drain, dry with paper toweling. Turn breast side down. Using sharp scissors and knife, carefully cut out wishbone from breast for easier carving. Preheat oven to 425 degrees.

2. Sprinkle inside with ½ t. salt. Tuck onion inside neck; bring skin of neck over back. Fasten with poultry pins. Stuff body cavity with garlic, black pepper and oranges. Close cavity with poultry pins. Tie legs together; bend wing tips under body.

3. Place on rack in shallow roasting pan. Pour ½ C. Burgundy over duckling. Roast, uncovered, 30 minutes. Reduce oven to 275 degrees; roast 1 ½ hours. Bring giblets to boiling in 2 cups water and ½ t. salt; reduce heat; simmer, covered, 1 hour. Strain.

4. Sauce: In a skillet into which you have put 2 T. butter, brown the liver. Remove from heat. Heat brandy slightly. Ignite the brandy and pour over liver. Remove liver, chop. In same skillet in rest of butter, sauté orange peel and garlic 3 minutes. Stir in flour, catsup, bouillon cube and pepper. (see next page)

5. Gradually add giblet broth, Burgundy, ¼ C. marmalade and the orange juice; mix well. Bring to boiling; reduce heat; simmer, stirring 15 minutes. Add liver and orange sections; heat. Spread duckling with ½ cup marmalade; roast 10 minutes longer.

6. Removes pins and twine. Place on heated platter. Using sharp knife, cut each side of breast into diagonal slices, ½ inch wide, starting at leg. Then run knife down center of breast to separate two sides; run knife around outer edge to cut skin. Pass sauce

CHICKEN CONTINENTAL

Brother, Mack and his wife, Mary sent me this chicken recipe and YUM!

1 can condensed cream of chicken soup
2 ½ T. grated onion
1 t. salt
Dash pepper
1 T. minced parsley

½ t. celery flakes
1/8 t. thyme
1 1/3 C. water
1 1/3 C. Minute Rice

For Chicken : 1 Cut up chicken; 1 Oven Fried Chicken coating; 1 Egg

1) Bake chicken according to Oven Fried coating instructions
2) Combine in sauce pan: 1 Can chicken soup   1 ½ t. grated onion
                         1 t. salt   Dash pepper
                         Minced parsley, celery flakes, thyme
   Mix all ingredients well.
3) Add one cup of water and mix well.
4) Bring to a boil, stirring constantly
5) Save 1/3 C. of soup mixture
6) Pour 1 1/3 uncooked Minute Rice into shallow 1 ½ qt. casserole
7) Pour remaining soup mixture over rice. Stir just enough to moisten all
8) Top with cooked chicken
9) Pour remaining 1/3 C. soup mixture over chicken
10) Cover and bake in a moderate oven (375 degrees) for about 20 minutes
11) Sprinkle with paprika if desired.

Serves 4

BREASTS OF CHICKEN DELUXE

5 Chicken breasts or 2 large, cut in half
1-1/2 C. flour
1 t. salt
½ t. pepper
1/3 C. butter
1 T. chopped onion

4 Oz. can mushrooms, drained
1 Chicken bouillon cube
1 C. hot water
¼ Cup cream
1 T. lemon juice
2 T. Sauterne wine (optional)

Coat chicken breasts in flour seasoned with salt and pepper. Brown slowly in melted butter, placing skin side down first. Remove chicken from pan; add onion and mushrooms and cook 2 to 3 minutes. Stir in 2 T. seasoned flour. Add hot water in which the bouillon cube is dissolved and stir until smooth. Add cream, lemon juice, and wine, stirring until smooth. Arrange chicken in casserole or flat baking dish. Spoon sauce and mushrooms over chicken. Cover. Bake in a pre-heated over at 350 degrees covered for about 1 hour; uncover chicken last 15 minutes to allow it to become crisp.

INTERNATIONAL CHICKEN

Use 6 boned chicken breasts
¼ C. butter
1 C. mandarin oranges
1 T. instant onion
½ t. curry powder
½ T. lemon juice

1 3/4 C. chicken broth
3 T. cornstarch
1 t. salt
1/8 t. pepper
1 C. pepper (slivered) if you like them.

Place breasts in shallow pan so pieces are touching. Brush well with melted butter and bake 350 degrees for 1 hour or until golden brown and fork tender. Drain oranges reserving syrup. Combine chicken broth and syrup in saucepan; blend in cornstarch. Add minced onion, salt, curry pepper and lemon juice. Cook until thickened and clear. Add green (or red/orange) pepper and heat for five minutes. Add dates and oranges. Pour over chicken, stirring into pan juices. I serve with steamed rice.

CHICKEN-WILD RICE CASSEROLE

2 Whole broiler-fryer
   Chickens, 3 Lb. each
1 C. water
1 C. dry sherry
½ t. salt
½ t. curry powder
1 Medium onion, sliced
½ C. sliced celery

1 lb. fresh mushrooms
¼ C. butter
2 Pkg. (6 oz. each) long
   grain wild rice with seasonings
1 C. dairy sour cream
1 C. condensed cream
mushroom soup

Place chickens in deep kettle. Add water, sherry, salt, curry powder, onion and celery. Bring to a boil; cover tightly. Reduce heat and simmer for 1 hour. Remove from heat and strain broth. Refrigerate chicken and broth at once. When chicken is cool, remove from bones, discard skin. Cut into bite sized pieces. Clean mushrooms and sauté in butter until golden brown (reserve enough to circle top of casserole). Measure chicken; use as part of liquid for cooking rice, following directions for cooking firm rice. Combine chicken, rice and mushrooms not used for top in a 3 ½ - 4 qt. casserole Blend sour cream and condensed cream of mushroom soup. Toss together with chicken mixture and arrange mushrooms in a circle on top. Cover; refrigerate. To bake, heat in a 350 oven for 1 hour. Serves 8-10.

ALMOND CHICKEN CASSEROLE

This is a great way to use leftover bird at Thanksgiving time. .

2 C. cooked and diced chicken or turkey
1 C. toasted cornflakes
½ C. toasted slivered almonds
½ C. shredded cheese of your choice
1 C. toasted cornflakes

¼ C. chopped onion
2 C. thin sliced celery
1 C. mayonnaise
2 T. Lemon juice
½ t. salt

Heat oven to 350 degrees. Combine all of the ingredients together except cheese and 1 C. cornflakes. Put in a 2 qt. casserole. Sprinkle with cheese and cornflakes. Bake 30 to 35 minutes. Stir. Top with remaining onions. Bake for 5 min. more. TIP: Toast ½ c. sliced almonds and add with remaining onions.

BEER CAN CHICKEN

I am made fun of for this recipe. I don't care, it's excellent in taste and beautiful when finished.

1 roaster chicken
1 can beer
Fresh thyme
Fresh rosemary
Fresh chives
1 lemon quartered
Olive oil to slather on the bird

Stuff the chicken with sprigs of fresh thyme, rosemary and chives. Add the lemon, quartered. Prop the chicken on a completely opened beer can i.e. take the entire top off or get a gizmo like I have that is engineered for such a feat. Preheat oven to 400 degrees and when you add the chicken turn it down to 350. Roast for and hour before checking it for doneness. If not done roast another ½ hour but keep checking your bird. It will be moist and most flavorful

BIG BUD'S BEER CAN CHICKEN

Guys make this recipe too!

1 Whole chicken
1 t. dried sage
1 t. dried oregano
1 t. sea salt
1 t. garlic powder
1 T. freshly ground black pepper

1 T. onion powder
2 Cloves garlic, smashed
1 t. paprika
1 (12 oz.) can beer
1 t. ground ginger
½ Lb. bacon

Preheat oven to 450 degrees. Wash chicken with cold water and pat dry with paper towels. Mix dry ingredient in small bowl. Rub ½ of the ingredients on inside cavity of chicken.

(Continued on next page)

Gently peel skin away from chicken and rub mixture into meat of chicken. Open beer can, pour out about ½ cup. Drop garlic cloves into the beer can. Place chicken, open end down, over the beer can to insert the beer into the cavity. Place chicken, standing up in large sauté pan. Place 1/3 of the bacon in the top cavity of the chicken and drape the remaining 2/3 of the bacon down the outside of the chicken. Pierce the bacon to the chicken with toothpicks.

Place chicken in the oven for 10 minutes and then lower the temperature to 325 degrees and cook for another 1 hour, or until the internal temperature in the thickest part of the thigh reaches 165 degrees on an instant-read thermometer.

OVEN LEMON CHICKEN

My mom's recipe file boasted this one and as I have mentioned before, my mama was a gourmand.

1 Fryer chicken cut into pieces (2 ½ to 3 Lb.)
1 C. flour
2 t. salt
1 t. paprika
6 T. butter

Basting Sauce:
¼ C. lemon juice
1 T. salad oil
½ t. each salt, thyme, garlic and onion

Coat chicken in flour/salt/paprika mixture. Melt butter in a baking pan; add chicken pieces and coat with butter evenly. Arrange in single layer. Bake at 375 for 30 minutes. Blend tog. ingredients for sauce. Turn chicken pieces and pour lemon sauce evenly over them. Continue baking until chicken is brown and tender about 30 minutes or more.

CHICKEN STRATA

This is Pat Shorey, Eppinga Goede's mother's recipe. Pat always had the best recipes!

8 C. diced cooked chicken
2 Large onions, chopped
2 Large green peppers, chopped
2 C. finely chopped celery
2 C. mayonnaise
2 T. salt

¼ t. pepper
32 Slices white bread, crusts removed
6 Eggs, slightly beaten
6 C. milk
4 Cans condensed mushroom soup
2 C. shredded sharp cheese

Dry bread in oven. Butter 8 slices and then cut in ½ inch cubes and set aside. Place 12 slices in bottom of 2 greased 13x9x2 pans. Combine first 7 ingredients; spoon over bread slices. Place remaining 12 bread slices on top. Combine egg and milk and pour over all. Cover and chill over night. Spoon soup over top. Sprinkle w/buttered cubes. Bake at 325 degrees – 50 to 60 minutes or until center is set. Sprinkle cheese over top last few minutes of baking.

- Serves 24   ¼ recipe serves 6 good portions in 8x8 pan.

CHICKEN CASSEROLE

5 C. cooked chicken, cubed
1 Pt. sour cream
1 Can cream of chicken soup
1 ½ C. Ritz crackers, crushed
1 Stick butter
1 Small can mushrooms
Poppy seeds

Mix the first three ingredients together. Sprinkle the crackers over top of casserole. Melt butter and sprinkle with poppy seeds. 9x13 pan. Bake 350 degrees for 30 minutes

CHICKEN SOUFFLE

3 Whole chicken breasts, boned and halved
Salt to taste
½ Lb. butter
6 Eggs separated
¼ C. Parmesan cheese, grated
4 Jumbo mushrooms, sliced

Preheat oven to 450 for individual casseroles or 375 for a shallow baking dish. Grease 6 individual casseroles or 1 shallow baking dish. Flatten chicken breasts with cleaver. Season lightly with salt. Melt butter over medium heat and sauté chicken breasts 5-7 minutes on each side. Beat egg whites until stiff and glossy, but not dry. Beat egg yolks until thick and lemon colored. Add Parmesan cheese to egg yolks and fold into whites. Arrange chicken breasts in prepared casseroles or baking dish. Lay mushrooms, slices around chicken, Spoon egg mixture over chicken bringing out to edges in individual casseroles 450 for 10 minutes. Bake in large dish at 375 for 15-20 minutes or until puffed and brown. Serve immediately.

MOLLIE FRIER'S CHICKEN DIVAN

2-10-ounce pkg. frozen broccoli
1 t. salt
1/4 C. water
2 C. sliced cooked chicken
2 C. condensed cream chicken soup
1 C. mayo.

½ T. lemon juice
½ t, curry powder
½ C. shredded cheese
½ C. bread crumbs
1 T. melted butter

Grease 12x9x2 inch casserole dish. Place chicken on broccoli. Add water and salt. Combine soup, mayo, lemon juice and curry; pour over chicken. Combine crumbs, cheese and butter; sprinkle over the top. Bake 350 degrees for 25-30 minutes   8 servings

CRESCENT TURKEY SQUARES

Preheat oven to 350. Blend 3 oz. softened cream cheese, 2 T. melted butter until smooth. Add 2 cups cooked cubed turkey, ¼ tsp. salt, 1/8 tsp. pepper, 2 T. milk 1 T. chopped chives or onion and mix well.

Separate 8 oz. can Pillsbury Refrigerator Crescent Dinner Rolls into 4 rectangles, seal perforations. Spoon ½ cup chicken mixture into center of each rectangle. Pull 4 corners of dough to center of mixture and seal.

Brush tops with 1 T. melted butter, dip in ½ cup crushed season croutons. Bake on ungreased cookies sheet 20 – 25 minutes until golden brown. Refrigerate any left overs. Makes 4

DEBRA BREY'S GRILLED CHICKEN W/ CANTALOUPE AND PINEAPPLE SALSA

2 T. lime juice
1 t. olive oil
½ t. salt
¼ t. ground black pepper
4 Boneless, skinless chicken breasts, halved

1 C. cantaloupe diced
½ C. chopped fresh pineapple or ½ c (8 oz) can crushed pineapple, drained
1/3 C. finely chopped red pepper
3 T. finely chopped red onion
1 T. finely chopped fresh cilantro
Cilantro sprigs (optional)

1) Heat grill
2) In medium size bowl, whisk together 1 T. lime juice, olive oil, salt and pepper to make marinade. Add chicken to marinade; toss to coat well. Cover and refrigerate 15 minutes.

(Continued on next page)

3) Meanwhile, make relish. In a small bowl, combine remaining 1 T. lime juice, cantaloupe, pineapple, red pepper, onion and cilantro. Cover and refrigerate until ready to use.
4) Grill chicken breasts.
5) To serve, place chicken breasts on cutting board; make 3 crosswise cuts on each to within 1 inch of opposite side, press to spread slices. Divide relish among chicken breasts.
Serves 4

TLC: Put seedless grapes in the freezer; they taste divine and it extends the life of them.

LOBSTER NEWBERG
ALA THE MUNROES, RON AND PENNY

This is not Cousin Penny's exact recipe but she and her husband, Ron, would together make this wonderful dish in their kitchen and serve it to very special guests like my cousin Margo and me. I wanted to offer this in their honor since every time I hear lobster Newberg, I think of the duo who resided in San Diego.

1 ½ C. cooked lobster meat   3 Egg yolks
4 T. butter (use the real stuff)   Salt
¼ C. brandy   Freshly ground pepper
1 C. heavy cream

Cut the lobster meat into large pieces and sauté in butter for 5 minutes. Add brandy and blaze. Mix the egg yolks and heavy cream together and heat in the upper part of a double boiler, stirring constantly until the mixture coats the spoon. Add the lobster and heat through, being careful not to let the mixture boil. Taste for seasoning. Serve in croustades, puff pastry shells or on rice.

LOBSTER THERMIDOR

I love lobster! Of course, it's expensive. Where did I get these over- the- top priced tastes? So, many times I fudge. Faux lobster (Louis Kemp) which I buy on sale and store in my big freezer does the trick for many main dishes and salads. It really is quite good. So this is what I use for this recipe. No groans, try it.

4 C. of lobster
2 Cans sliced mushrooms (4 oz. each)
¼ C. butter
1 t. prepared mustard
2 T. Minced parsley

1 ½ C. fine cracker crumbs
1 Can cream of mushroom soup
½ C. sherry, optional
3 T. Grated Parmesan cheese

Cut the "lobster" meat into small pieces. Saute mushrooms in butter; add mustard, parsley, crackers, soup and sherry; blend well, then stir in lobster meat. Use oven proof mini-casserole dishes (4), Fill with mixture, sprinkle with cheese and bake in hot oven 450 degrees, 10 to 15 minutes or until thoroughly heated.

SHRIMP CASSEROLE

This recipe came from Jean Murphy, married to Bob and mother of five. She was a superb homemaker besides being beautiful and cooked up a storm. Scrumptious!

1 tablespoon butter or margarine
1 medium sweet onion, sliced thin
1 clove garlic crushed
1 can cream mushroom soup

1 cup sour cream
¼ cup catsup
1 4 oz. can mushrooms, drained
2 cups cleaned shrimp

Cook shrimp. Saute onion and garlic in butter till tender. Combine soup, sour cream and catsup and combine with onions. Add shrimp and mushrooms. Cook over low heat til mixture is heated through. Serve over rice.

TUNA NOODLE CASSEROLE

I think that everyone who was Catholic in the bygone days searched for a good recipe for anything tuna for Friday night's meal . . . here's one from Mack and Mary Margrave.

2 Cans condensed cream of mushroom soup
1 C. milk
2 C. frozen peas
2 Cans (12 oz. each) tuna in water, drained
4 C. of hot cooked medium egg noodles
2 T. dry bread crumbs
1 t. melted butter

Stir soup, milk, peas, tuna and noodles in 3 qt. casserole. Bake at 400° for 30 minutes or until hot. Stir. Mix bread crumbs with butter and sprinkle over the tuna mixture. Bake for 10 minutes more. Serves 6

CREVETTES AU CHAMIGNON, AMANDINE

Back in the early sixties, I belonged to two guilds which supported the needs of both Butterworth and St. Mary's Hospitals in Grand Rapids, Michigan. As a money maker, Porter Guild of Butterworth was about to published a cookbook. Its membership raced to offer her most impressive recipes. This one sounds a little uppity, but is not difficult to make and is wonderfully tasty.

½ C. wild rice
½ C. white rice
½ C. chopped celery
½ C. chopped green pepper
1 C. chopped onion

1 Box mushrooms
1 Can mushroom soup, undiluted
2 Lbs. cooked shrimp
1 Can crab
Sharp cheese

Cook rice separately in salt water. Saute celery, green pepper, onion and mushrooms in plenty of butter. Season with salt and pepper. Combine all ingredients in a casserole. Cover with a goodly amount of sharp grated cheese. Make 1 ½ cups of medium white sauce and pour on top of cheese. Do not stir. Saute ¼ pound almond halves and sprinkle on top. Bake 40 minutes at 325 degrees.

SHRIMP DE JONGHE

Oh so scrumptious

2 quarts water
2 stalks celery, tops and all
2 carrots, sliced
2 small onions, diced
Juice of one lemon
2 t. salt
1 t. black pepper, freshly ground
1 sprig parsley
1 bay leaf

2 pounds of shrimp, shelled and deveined
large clove garlic
¾ cup butter
1 t. salt
A pinch of tarragon
A pinch of marjoram
1 cup fine bread crumbs
½ cup dry sherry
Parsley, chopped

In a large saucepan bring two quarts of water to a boil; add celery, carrots, onions, lemon juice, salt, pepper, spring of parsley and bay leaf. Simmer for 15 minutes. Add the shrimp and simmer, uncovered, until pink, 2 to 5 minutes. You can either drain or leave the shrimp in the broth until assembling dish.

In a mixing bowl, mash garlic with back of spoon until almost paste. Add butter, softened to room temperature, the salt, tarragon and marjoram. Cream them together until well blended, then add bread crumbs and dry sherry. Blend well. In a large buttered baking dish, place alternate layers of the shrimp and bread crumb mixture, sprinkling chopped parsley over the top of each layer. Bake in a 400 degree oven for 20 to 25 minutes and serve immediately. Serves 6

DILL SAUCE

great with salmon

2 C. sour cream
½ t. salt
¼ t. pepper
1 T. Chopped dill or 1 ½ tsp. dried
2 T. Snipped chives or green onions
¾ C. Coarsely chopped cucumber, drained well.

Mix and refrigerate until ready for use.

OVEN BAKED COD

½ C. oil
1 ½ C. dry bread crumbs
½ t. dry dill weed, dry basil or dry Italian herbs
1 ½ Lbs. skinless cod fillet
1 T. vegetable oil

Preheat oven to 400. Pour crumbs into a plate and mix with dill. Rinse fish and pat dry, cut across to 2-inch strips. Pour oil in another plate. Soak pieces of fish in oil, allow excess to drip off, then coat in crumbs to cover all sides. Arrange breaded strips of cod on a baking sheet with about 1 inch between pieces. Bake until fish is opaque in center (cut to test) 8-10 minutes.

Serves 4-6

AUNT AUDREY BEEBE'S BAGGED FISH FILLETS

My father's family was raised Methodist. The women followed the tradition in which they were raised. One year the local church in Whitehall published a cookbook and so this was Aunt Audrey's contribution.

1 T. flour
1 Small onion, chopped
2 T. chopped celery
1 Lb. frozen, skinless ocean perch
    or haddock fillets

4 T. firm butter
¾ t. salt
1/8 t. sweet basil
¼ t. thyme
3 T. lemon juice

Shake flour in 10x16 cooking bag and place in 2-inch deep roasting pan. Place ¼ of onion and celery in bottom of bag and top with frozen fish block. Dot with small chunks of butter, sprinkle with seasonings, lemon juice and remaining vegetables. Close bag with a twist tie and make 6 ½ slits in top. Bake at 375 degrees for 25-30 minutes or until fish flakes easily. About 5 minutes before fish is done, press on block gently from outside of bag with wooden spoon to partially separate fillets. Shake bag gently to splash juice over fish. Continue cooking. Serves 4.

MICROWAVE FLOUNDER FLORENTINE

1 Clove garlic, minced or pressed
4 oz. mushrooms, thinly sliced
2 T. finely chopped onion
1 t. olive oil
1 10 Oz pkg. frozen chopped spinach, thawed and squeezed dry
4 Flounder or sole fillets (about 4 oz. each)

2 T. grated parmesan cheese
2 t. Dijon-style mustard
Salt and pepper

Combine garlic, mushrooms, onion and olive oil in a microwave safe bowl, cover and microwave on high (100% power) for 2 minutes, stirring once, drain liquid. Add cheese, mustard, salt, pepper and spinach and mix well. Rinse fish and pat dry. Lay fillets on work surface, nice looking side down. Spread spinach mixture over, leaving 1 inch clear at each end. Roll up beginning at thicker end and set seam side down in a lightly oiled microwave baking dish. Cover and microwave on high until opaque through center (cut to test) 4-5 minutes. Rotate dish a quarter turn halfway through cooking time. Let fish stand, covered, for a few minutes before serving.

PAN FRIED SOLE

¾ Lb. sole fillets, about ¼ inch thick
Salt and pepper
1/3 C. dried bread crumbs or flour

1 T. olive oil
½ t. Paprika
1 Lemon

Rinse fish and pat dry. Cut fillets to fit frying pan, if needed. Lightly season with salt and pepper. Combine crumbs and paprika in shallow dish. Dip fillets into crumbs, turn to thoroughly coat them and then shake off excess. Squeeze juice from ½ lemon. Cut remaining half into wedges. Heat oil (I would throw in some added butter) in frying pan over medium heat, preferably non-stick pan. Lay fish in pan without overlapping them. Cook them until edges become opaque and bottom is browned 2-3 minutes. Carefully turn them over and cook until opaque through center, 1-2 minutes more. Transfer fish to plates and cover to keep warm All lemon juice to pan and boil to thicken, about 30 seconds, scraping up cooked bits. Pour sauce over fish and garnish with lemon wedges.
Serves 2

GRILLED MONKFISH

I really like monkfish, called 'the poor man's lobster'-- and it does indeed taste like lobster. A poor man in today's world however, cannot afford Monkfish. This is a most unique fish that is thick and grills beautifully.

Can be prepared ahead and serves 4

4 Pieces of Monkfish
1 Bottle Italian dressing
Salt and pepper to taste

1 Stick butter, melted
¼ C. lemon juice, fresh
    squeezed

Wash and dry pieces of fish. Place in a large glass baking dish and pour dressing evenly over each fish. Sprinkle salt and freshly ground pepper. Let marinate for at least 1 hour.

When grill is very hot, place fish on rack and cover. Cook on each side 6 to 10 minutes, turning only once. Just before fish are done, mix melted butter and lemon juice and drizzle over fish.

CRISPY MONKFISH FILLETS

1 Lb. Monkfish fillets
¼ to ½ C. Dijon mustard
½ t. salt
½ t. cracked pepper
½ C. flour

1 Egg, slightly beaten
2 T. milk
½ C. vegetable oil for cooking
1 Lemon sliced for garnish
3-6 Springs of fresh parsley

Slice fillets in strips 3-4 inches long and approximately 1 inch thick. Coat each fillet strip generously with Dijon mustard, season with salt and pepper and dip lightly into flour. Dip fillets into an egg wash (made by combining egg and milk) and redip lightly in flour. Shake off excess flour. Fry in 375- degree oil for 3-4 minutes or until fillets are golden and fish is tender. Do not overcook. Garnish with lemon slices and fresh parsley.

Serve with scalloped potatoes and fresh greens   Serves 4

RED SNAPER PARMESAN

2 Lb. red snapper (or other white fish), dressed
1 C. sour cream
¼ C. Grated Parmesan cheese
1 T. lemon juice
1 T. grated onion
1 t. salt
Dash hot red pepper sauce
Paprika

Preheat oven to 350. Grease baking dish. Cut fish into serving size pieces. Place in baking dish. Combine other ingredients except paprika. Spread over fish. Sprinkle with paprika. Bake 25 to 30 minutes.   Yields: 6 servings

FRIED PERCH COATING

Early in the 1980's, my mother and brother together owned a place on Scenic Drive in Whitehall, MI called the Red Rooster. When they took it over, it became magic. Great jazz on Sunday afternoons abounded where one couldn't get a seat, it was so crowded. Perch was served on Friday nights and one waited for seats for that too. One of the women who worked there thought that she had cracked the recipe for fish coating. I am not too sure, but I will share it with you.

5 C. flour
4 T. seasoned salt
Grind together 3 Lb. soda crackers and 1 Lb. cheese crackers
Mix all together. Dip fish in an egg wash, then the coating before deep frying.

SPINACH SOUFFLE

This recipe comes from my darling Grandmother Robarge's 1932
Detroit Times Cook Book.

Boil spinach, drain well and press through a course mesh sieve into; about 1 cup of spinach pulp is left. (I am sure that one could use frozen spinach, cooked per directions).

Heat one T. butter in a saucepan, season and stir in the spinach. Stir in yolks of 3 eggs one at a time. Remove from flame and when cool, beat in ¼ C. whipped cream. Beat the whites of the eggs still and fold in the spinach. Grease a souf-flé dish. Turn in the spinach and bake in a moderate oven (325 degrees) for one hour. Serve immediately so that the puffy soufflé will not fall.

SQUASH CASSEROLE

I was visiting my brother, Mack, in Atlanta where he was playing in the 70's and met one of his delightfully fun and talented friends, singer Deanie Mustin. She called Mack, "precious". She was a real southern cook and gave me this recipe. The casserole was so good I had to stop myself from licking the dish so as not to embarrass my dear brother.

2 C. cooked mashed squash (freezer has it)
1 Medium onion
2 Stalks celery
1 t. salt
½ Stick butter
2 Slices bread, cubed and browned in butter
1 Beaten egg
Chop celery and onion. Add salt and sauté until tender and add to squash. Throw into a food processor, add other ingredients except cracker crumbs and pulsate a few times until incorporated. Finally pour into a buttered casserole dish. Then you may cover with the buttered cracker crumbs and bake at 350 degrees for 30 minutes. Serves 6.

GERMAN POTATO PANCAKES

6 Medium baking potatoes
2 Eggs, beaten
¼ C. onion, finely grated

1/3 C. oatmeal
1 t. salt
Vegetable oil

Peal potatoes: drop into cold water to prevent discoloring. In large bowl, combine eggs and onions, gradually beat in oatmeal and salt. Pat potatoes dry; grate coarsely into a sieve. Press out as much moisture as possible. Immediately stir into egg mixture. Pan fry until golden. 14 pancakes

LATKES

to be served with Florence Obstfeld's son's brisket

5 Potatoes
¼ Med. onion
1 Egg
¼ C. Bisquick or more
Salt
Pepper
Oil

Grate potatoes and onions. Put in strainer and press to get rid of water. Put excess water in a bowl. Let sit for about 10 minutes. Pour off water and put starch back into potato mixture. Beat egg and mix w/potatoes. Add salt and pepper.

Heat lots of oil in a frying pan. When hot, add a large spoonful of potato mixture. Squash with spoon. Fry until edges turn brown. Turn over and fry till golden brown. Can cook about 4 pancakes in a pan at a time. Drain on paper towels. Keep warm in oven while making batch. Serve with apple sauce or sour cream.

FRIED GREEN TOMATOES

1 C. milk or buttermilk if you have it
1 C. diced cheddar cheese
Dash Tabasco
1 T. Worcestershire sauce
¼ t. paprika
1 C. all-purpose flour
½ C. cornmeal
2 C. cooking oil

1 to 3 Medium green tomatoes (about 1 lb.) sliced 3/8 inch thick
In a 10- inch skillet, heat the 2 cups cooking oil over medium high heat
In a medium bowl, combine egg, water, the 1 tablespoon cooking oil, the salt, and pepper. Add ½ cup of the flour; beat with a wire whisk until smooth. Set aside. In a shallow bowl, combine remaining flour and cornmeal; set aside.

Dip green tomato slices, one at a time, into egg mixture, then into the cornmeal mixture, coating both sides of each slice. Cook the coated tomato slices, a few at a time, in the hot cooking oil for 4 to 5 minutes or until coating is golden brown; turn once during cooking.

Keep fried tomato slices warm in a 300 degree oven while frying remaining slices. Season to taste. Makes 4 – 6 side dish servings A relish is wonderful over them.

CRUNCHY-TOP SWEET POTATO SOUFFLE

Many years ago I found this superb recipe in the Cook and Love It cook book my brother, Mack Margrave had given me. As a professional musician, he inhabited Atlanta for lots of years and had friends whose kids went to the Lovett School from where the book had its origin. The entire book has been enchanting all these years but this one recipe sort of took the prize and every Thanksgiving ever since, it has been laid on the table for guests to enjoy.

3 C. sweet potatoes, mashed
2 Eggs, lightly beaten
½ C. milk
1 t. vanilla

1 C. sugar
½ t. salt
1/3 Stick butter

Topping

1/3 Stick butter
1/3 C. flour

1 C. brown sugar
1 C. nuts (pecans or walnuts)

Mix together all ingredients except topping and beat until fluffy and all potato strings removed. Pour into greased baking dish. Melt butter. Add brown sugar, flour and pecans. Pour over sweet potatoes. Bake at 350 degrees for 35 minutes

CURRIED FRUIT

1 Large can peaches
1 Large can pears
1 Large can chunk pineapple

1 Can apricots
1 Jar maraschino cherries

Drain the above.

½ C. brown sugar
2 t. curry powder

1/3 C. butter

Boil the 3 above ingredients and pour over fruit. Put in a 9 x 13 pan and refrigerate 24 hours. Bake 325 for 1 hour uncovered. Great with ham, chicken and breakfast fare too.

CHARLIE MARGRAVEY

This recipe is almost one hundred years old. It was named for my father, Charles Margrave, by his four older sisters who were in themselves extraordinary cooks. I have modified it as the years rolled by and proudly present this up to date version. An easy stuffing extravaganza for your holiday bird.

1 16 oz. package of herbed Pepperidge Farm stuff
2 ½ C. of chicken or vegetable broth – found in the soup section
1 Stick of butter (1/4 pound), melted
¼ C. olive oil
1 C. celery, sliced
1 C. onions, chopped
1 8 oz. package of sliced fresh mushrooms
1 ½ C. shredded cheddar cheese
1 C. of pecans, chopped
1 C. of dried cranberries of cherries

Saute the celery, onions and mushrooms in an olive oil until limp; add the pecans and give them a twirl. While they are cooking, in a large bowl mix the stuffing, broth and melted butter. Use your hands (come on, it's fun) to incorporate the dried cranberries or cherries as well as the sautéed mixture after it has cooled. Don't forget the cheese for this is what makes it Charlie Margravey. Stuff your bird in both cavities with the mixture. You will have some leftovers which may be placed in a greased, covered dish and baked for ½ hour at 325 degrees. Enjoy!

CINDY BOARDWELL PRICE'S
GREEN BEAN STIR FRY

Cindy is the younger of the Boardwell girls. She is the twin to her mirror, Debra and Doug followed both of them a few years later. Cindy fixes this dish during the Thanksgiving holidays because her brother likes it and so I asked her if she would share it and she graciously agreed.

4 Cans of green and yellow cut beans
½ Lb. bacon
1 Shallot, diced

Cut bacon into bite size pieces with a sharp knife or scissors. Slowly fry them in a pan. When they look as though they are done, add the diced shallot and scramble it around until it is wilted. Then throw in the drained cans of beans and heat thoroughly. I recommend also throwing in 1 tsp. sugar (just for good luck). Just because Julia says so.

THE CLASSIC GREEN BEAN CASSEROLE

2 Cans (10 ¾ oz. each) Campbell's Condensed Cream of Mushroom Soup
1 C. milk
2 t. soy sauce
¼ t. ground black pepper
8 C. cooked cut green beans
1 Can (6 oz.) French's French Fried Onions (2 2/3 cups)

1. Stir soup, milk, soy sauces, pepper, beans and 1 1/3 cups onions in 3-qt. casserole.
2. Bake at 350 degrees for 25 minutes or until hot. Stir.
3. Top with remaining onions. Bake for 5 min. more.

TIP: Toast ½ c. sliced almonds and add with remaining onions.

AUNT LORNA'S EGGPLANT FRITTERS

Who knows if Aunt Lorna devised this recipe or not. She had the cook, Miss Pontias, the houseboy, Jimmy as well as a nurse for cousin Penny. She did love to entertain and excelled at it. Here is one offering from her recipe file,

2 T. flour
1 Egg, beaten
3 C. cooked eggplant, mashed
½ t. salt
Dash pepper
Fat for deep frying

Stir flour and egg into the eggplant. Beat until very light. Season. Drop by tablespoons into hot fat (375) and fry until brown. Serves 6 – 8. (editor's note. I might also add some shredded Parmesan cheese to add another of dimensional flavor).

BETTY ADAMS CRANBERRY SAUCE

I would eat with great gusto anything this woman made. She was a natural. Since receiving this recipe, I have made it almost every Thanksgiving.

1 Lb. cranberries
2 ½ C. sugar
1 C. chopped walnuts
1 C. orange marmalade
Juice of one lemon or lime

Sort, wash and drain cranberries. Put in shallow baking pan and stir in sugar lightly. Cover with lid or foil and bake at 325 degrees for 1 hour. Put in walnuts during last 10minutes. Add marmalade and juices and mix well. Chill.

MARINATED CARROTS

I gave these once to a friend and coworker at Barnes and Noble who had broken a wrist and an ankle and was a vegan (I think). It was difficult to come up with something that I thought she could nibble on and enjoy. She did and she did.

5 Carrots, cut in 1-in. pieces
1 Red Onion, diced
1 Can tomato soup
1 C. sugar
1 t. salt

1 t. prepared mustard
1 Red or yellow pepper, diced
½ C. salad oil
¼ C. cider vinegar
1 t. pepper

Cook carrots until just tender; drain. Add onions and peppers to carrots. Combine the rest of ingredients; cook until hot, Pour hot over carrots, onions and peppers. Marinate in frig over night.

BLENDER HOLLANDAISE SAUCE

3 Egg yolks
1/4 t. salt
1 to 2 T. lemon juice

Dash Tabasco sauce
1 Stick butter

Put egg yolks, lemon juice and cayenne pepper in blender. Blend for 3 seconds on high. While continuing to blend, melt butter to bubbling and add in a steady stream. Keep warm over hot water.

Cousin Penny and Ron serve artichokes with mayonnaise and a little fresh lemon drizzled into it for a hollandaise sauce effect.

A darned good chef I know buys hollandaise sauce in a packet and adds fresh lemon to it along with the prescribed directions. I'll stick with Julia.

I am passionate about Chinese food and have a cookbook which shares 1001 recipes. I am going to share my Auntie Greet's wonderful Chop Suey recipe and then give you Egg Foo Yung which is a real favorite followed by Hum Bao which can be bought off the street in Seattle's Pike Place Market (once I was introduced to this edible by my very best friend, Donna Driscoll Brancheau, I was hooked and found this recipe I share with you). Another favorite is Chinese Chicken Walnut given to me by an old college pal, now gone from us, who was a wonderfully creative cook.

CHOP SUEY
Auntie Greet's very old, very good recipe

1 Lb. stew meat (pork, veal, or beef)
1 C. chopped celery
1 C. chopped onion
Brown slowly in pan
Add 2 C. water and cook until ½ of the water remains.
Add 1 can bean sprouts, drained

Mix thinkening ingredients: 2 T. Flour, salt, 2 T. Molasses, 2 T. Soy sauce.
Add thickening to the mixture above and stir well.
Serve over rice.

LEFT OVER RICE

I was always fascinated with sizzling rice dishes at the Chinese restaurants. It took a lot of digging but I found out how they make it. Bring home left over rice from the restaurant or use the left over rice that has stuck to the bottom of a pan you are using. Patted down, it is sort of a crust that can be preserved in the frig until you want to use it. Break into smaller chunks and deep fry it. It can be used in sizzling rice dishes or as munchies. I just love it.

SHRIMP EGG FOO YUNG

– 4 servings. MSG may be eliminated if allergies are in question.

4 Eggs
½ C. cooked shrimp
1 C. fresh or canned bean sprouts, drained
¼ C. chopped onions
¼ C. chopped fresh mushrooms

1 Scallion, chopped
1 T. soy sauce
1 t. salt
½ t. sugar
4 T. peanut or corn oil

Preparation: Beat the 4 egg thoroughly. Cut shrimp into small pieces. With 1 T. oil, sauté the onions, mushrooms, and scallion for 1 minute. Add bean sprouts and shrimps. Then add 1 T. soy sauce, 1 t. salt and 1 t. sugar. Mix well. Place in dish and let cool. Then combine beaten eggs with cooled cooked mixture.

Cooking: Using a frying pan 4" in diameter, heat 2 t. oil over low flame. When oil is hot, ladle in about ¼ the egg mixture. Cook until eggs have browned on one side. Turn over and brown the other side. Place in dish and set aside. Repeat this process, adding oil as necessary until eggs are used up.

Ingredients for sauce:

½ C. clear chicken broth
1 t. soy sauce
½ t. salt

¼ t. MSG
2 t. cornstarch

Cooking Sauce: Bring to boil ½ C. chicken broth and add 1 t. soy sauce, ½ t. salt and ¼ tsp. MSG. Dissolve 2 t.. cornstarch in 1 T. cold water and gradually stir into other sauce until it thickens.

Pour sauce over pancakes and serve hot. Makes 4-5 pancakes.

Note: The egg portion of this recipe can be prepared early in the day and reheated later in a double boiler or oven. The sauce, however should be made just before serving to get best results. Shreds of roast port, roast beef, chicken or turkey can all be substituted for the shrimp.

SHRIMP FRIED RICE

Everyone's favorite - - - -and a great way to use up leftovers. Try this with 4 Oz. diced leftover chicken, turkey or Chinese roast pork instead of shrimp. The secret to perfect fried rice is to start with cold rice—and to serve the dish immediately after cooking to prevent sogginess. Have all ingredients chopped and ready ahead of time; actual cooking takes less than 5 minutes.

1 Egg	½ C. diced celery
3 Egg whites	1 Minced clove garlic
1 T. peanut oil	
1 C. finely chopped scallions (white and green parts)	
24 peeled cooked small shrimp	1 C. thawed frozen peas
3 ½ C. cooked brown rice	1 T. soy sauce

1) In small bowl, beat together egg and egg whites; set aside.
2) Place large nonstick saucepan or wok over medium high heat 30 seconds. Add oil; heat 30 seconds. Add scallions, celery and garlic; cook, stirring constantly until soft, about 5 minutes
3) Reduce heat to medium low; add beaten eggs and cook. Stirring gently until set, 1 minute. Stir in shrimp and peas; cook, tossing lightly, until heated through, 2 minutes. Add rice and continue tossing lightly until heated through, 2 minutes. Sprinkle with soy sauce and toss lightly; serve immediately.   Yields 6 servings.

JIM HOLMBLADE'S SWEET SOUR SAUCE
He was such a grand cook!

¼ C. catsup
¼ C. sugar
1 C. water
¼ C. white vinegar
2 T. cornstarch dissolved in 2 T. water
½ Green pepper, diced
1 T. crushed pineapple (canned)
1) Combine first 4 ingredients in saucepan. Bring to boil.
2) Thicken with dissolved cornstarch. Stir constantly.
3) Add green pepper and pineapple. Stir.

May be refrigerated or frozen.

CHINESE CHICKEN WALNUT

An old college friend gave this recipe to me many years ago. I think that he loved to cook as much as I. We made this great recipe together and I have made it many times since. He has left us but how wonderful he left this remembrance behind.

1 Whole boned chicken
2 C. ham
1 C. broken walnuts.

Marinade: 5 T. oil
                         ½ t. sugar
                         2 T. corn starch
                         Salt and pepper to taste
                         5 T. soy sauce

Add chicken and let settle after coating

Saute walnuts until golden. Brown chicken after marinating process.
Mix and add ½ C. chicken bouillon. Simmer 20minutes.
Serve over brown rice

YEN CHING'S SAUTED SHRIMP

Jack and Mary who owned Yen Ching in Grand Rapids which served fabulous dishes gave me this marvelous recipe for an appetizer. Eating this dish with your fingers, you sort of suck on the shrimp to ensure that you reach the full flavor, then chew. Divine!

4 cups jumbo shrimp, unpeeled
¼ cup corn oil
Seasoning: 1 T. light soy
                         ½ t. white pepper
                         1 T. minced scallion
                         1 T. grated fresh ginger root
                         2 t. rice wine vinegar or dry sherry
                         1 t. salt
Marinate shrimp in marinade for 30 minutes and stir fry until pink. Peel. Serve immediately.

MOO SHOO PORK PANCAKES

I think that I came upon this dish came in the late 1970's or early '80's. I was hooked! Use chicken, shrimp or tofu if you wish, but do try these.

2 ½ cups all-purpose flour (reserve ¼ cup+2 t. for prep area
1 cup boiling water

1) Lightly dust 2 baking sheets with 2 t. of reserved flour; set aside.

2) In large bowl or food processor, combine flour and boiling water and mix well, or process 1 minute. Let cool 2 minutes. If mixing by hand, sprinkle work surface with 2 T. of the reserved flour, turn dough out onto prepared surface and knead until smooth and elastic, 7 – 8 minutes.

3) Divide dough in half; cover 1 half with plastic wrap; roll remaining dough half into a log, about 12" long and 1 ½ " wide.
Cut into 8 equal pieces. Sprinkle work surface with 2 tablespoons or the reserved flour and turn out dough pieces on work surface.

4) With your fingers, on prepared work surface, flatten 1 dough piece into a 2" diameter circle; spray top with non-stick cooking spray. Flatten another piece of dough and press on top of the first. Roll with rolling pin to make one 5" diameter thin pancake. Place on prepared baking sheet; cover with plastic wrap. Repeat with remaining dough pieces to make 4 pancakes. Sprinkle work surface with remaining 2 tablespoons reserved flour and repeat process with other dough half, to make 4 more pancakes.

5) Heat non-stick skillet over medium high heat until a drop of water dances across its surface. Add 1 pancake and cook, shaking pan to rotate pancake as it cooks, until puffy in center, about 1 minute. Turn and repeat other side, until lightly browned on both sides (watch for burning). Remove to plate and repeat with remaining pancakes. When pancakes have cooled slightly, peel them apart to make 16 pancakes. Cover with plastic wrap and refrigerate.

MOO SHOO PORK (chicken, shrimp or tofu)

16 Medium scallions
1 Egg
3 Egg whites
1 t. peanut oil
1 Minced garlic clove
One ¼ inch piece pared fresh ginger root, minced
2 ½ C. thinly sliced green cabbage
8 Dried Chinese mushroom caps, reconstituted in hot water, drained and thinly
    sliced, or 2 C. thinly sliced fresh mushrooms.
½ C. drained rinsed canned bamboo shoots, sliced into matchstick-size strips
1 t. soy sauce
1 t. sesame oil
¼ t. Chinese 5-spice powder
16 Moo Shoo Pancakes or twelve 1 – ounce flour tortillas, halved
2 T + 2 t. Hoisin sauce

1) To make scallion brushes, fill medium bowl with water and ice cubes. Trim
tops off scallions, leaving 1" of green, finely chop green tops and set aside. With
sharp snife, make several vertical cuts starting at green end of scallion bases.
Cutting down towards bulb and stopping where white part begins. Place in ice
water and set aside to "curl."
2) In small bowl, beat together egg and egg whites; set aside.
3) Place large nonstick saucepan or wok over medium-high heat 30 seconds.
Add peanut oil, heat 30 seconds. Add the minced scallion tops, the garlic and
ginger , cook until scallions are soft, 5-8 , minutes. Add cabbage, mushrooms
and bamboo shoots; stir-fry until browned, about 10 minutes. Add pork (or
chicken or shrimp or tofu), the beaten eggs, soy sauce, sesame oil and 5-spice
powder; cook , stirring, until eggs are cooked, 3-4 minutes. Remove from heat
and set aside.
4) Meanwhile, steam pancakes or tortillas; Layer pancakes or tortillas between
sheets of damp paper towels on a microwave safe plate; microwave 4 at a time
on medium 30 seconds. Wrap steamed pancakes in a cloth napkin.

5) To serve, drain scallion brushes and use each brush to spread ½ t. hoisin sauce in the center of each steamed pancake. Top each with ¼ cup of the pork mixture and the scallion brush; fold over edges of pancake like an envelope to enclose filling.

HUM BAO BUNS

I was introduced to this wonderful treat on the streets of Seattle in Pike Place Market by my best friend, Donna Driscoll Brancheau. These little dim sums are very addictive so I was delighted when I found a recipe.

For the barbecue pork

1 C. firmly packed brown sugar
¼ C. ketchup
2 T. soy sauce
2 T. Hoisin sauce

1 T. dry sherry
1 Garlic clove, minced
1½ Lb. pork steaks – ½ inch thick

Sauce

1 T. corn starch
1 T. dry sherry
1 T. soy sauce
½ C. chicken broth

½ C. chopped water chestnuts
1 T. peanut or vegetable oil
½ C. chopped onion

Pastry: 1 (17.3 oz.) can large refrigerator buttermilk biscuits
Glaze: 1 t. sugar, 1 Egg white, 1 t. water

Heat oven 375 degrees. Line broiler pan with foil. In blender container or food processor bowl with metal blade, combine all roast pork ingredients except the pork. Blend until smooth. Generously brush both sides of pork steak, reserving remaining basting sauce. Place pork steaks on foil lined broiler pan.

Bake at 375 degrees for 30 minutes. Remove from oven. Brush sides of steak with remaining basting sauce. Bake an additional 10 – 20 minutes or until no longer pink in center. Remove from oven, cool- leave oven on. Remove meat from bones and finely chop – set aside. In small bowl, combine cornstarch and 1 T. sherry. Blend well. Heat oil in lg. skillet over high heat. Add onion and water chestnuts, cook and stir 2 – 3 minutes until onion begins to brown, add 1 T. soy sauce, 1 T. Hoisin, then stir to coat.

Add broth, stir in corn starch mixture, cool and stir until mixture begins to thicken. Remove from heat and stir in pork. Separate dough into 8 biscuits on lightly flowered surface, press or roll each biscuit into 5 inch circles. Place about ½ C. pork mixture in center of each biscuit. Gather up edges, twist and pinch to seat. Place seam side down on ungreased cookie sheet. In small bowl, beat glaze ingredients until well blended. Brush over buns. Bake @ 375 for 14 – 18 minutes , until golden brown.   Yield: 8 servings

CHINESE BUN DOUGH

If you must make your own buns for the Hum Bao, here is a recipe to do so. This recipe calls for steaming, but I bake 'em. – makes 8 servings

2 ½ t. dry yeast
1 t. sugar
1 C. of lukewarm water
3 C. all-purpose flour (reserve 1 T. if mixing by hand)

1) In a small bowl, sprinkle yeast and sugar evenly over the lukewarm water; stir until yeast dissolves. Let stand 10 minutes or until foamy.
2) In large bowl or food processor, combine flour and yeast mixture and mix well, or process 1 minute. If mixing by hand, sprinkle work surface with the reserved 1 tablespoon flour; turn dough out onto work surface and knead until dough is smooth and elastic, about 10 minutes.
3) Spray large bowl with nonstick cooking spray; place dough in bowl. Cover loosely with plastic wrap or damp towel and let rise until dough triples in volume, about 3 hours. Punch down and wrap in plastic until ready to use. Will keep for 3 days in refrigerator and up to 2 months in freezer.

ORIENTAL RICE – A side dish

I'm not sure from whence this recipe came, but it popped up on my kitchen counter in the 60's and I really liked the flavor. You will too if you enjoy Asian cooking. You must top it with something interesting like a greenery of some sorts: chopped chives, flat leaf parsley or the likes for I took this concoction along with two little Brey boys and their father to a church potluck and not one soul tried my dish. . It had no allure! No greenery! In one way I was glad, because I could take it back home, and eat from it for lunch, but it was a little embarrassing since so many of the homemakers dishes were empty. If one doesn't try the culinary assets of a dish, one never expands the pallet for varied and ethnic sorts of foods. Therefore here is another rice dish.

Two C. uncooked rice   2 Envelopes brown gravy mix or jars of same
1 t. salt   2 Shallots minced finely,
1 cup sliced mushrooms & 1 minced garlic , sautéed in butter
1 Qt. of water

Cook the above until completely done
Then add 1 T. Soy sauce, taste and correct according to directions on package, seasoning to your taste

Prepare brown gravy mixture according to pkg. directions while shallots, mushrooms and garlic are sautéing. Mix everything together and heat through.
Throw greenery on top for décor.

Serves 8

GREEK STUFF

When my oldest son, Hal, was graduating from high school, he went to a lot of celebratory parties. One such was hosted by his Greek friend and fellow Pro-ton, Terry Zerfis' parents who served home made Greek food. Hal raved and smiled and smiled and raved. I wanted to make a Greek feast of my own for him at Christmas time the following year so I took a class in Greek cooking at community education and had a blast. I am going to offer here pasticcio, mousaka, and spanakopitta. The baklavah is found in the dessert section. Yes, we made all of these and more but this is enough to give you for a challenge. Go ahead, you can do it. . .it just takes lots of time.

MOUSAKA

By way of introduction, mousaka is an extraordinarily versatile dish, as it can be made with potatoes, eggplant, zucchini or a mixture or all three (or two). The only rule to remember is that the potatoes must be either fried or boiled somewhat and the eggplant and zucchini must, similarly, be either broiled or fried. Otherwise you will come out with vegetables that are not done in the casserole. The version that follows uses potatoes:

1 Sliced onion	1- 1 Lb. can tomatoes
2 Cloves garlic	1 Bay leaf
1 C. butter	Salt and pepper
1 Lb. ground round	2 ½ Lbs. potatoes

Optional, but instructor suggests 2 eggs

Sauce ingredients

4 T. butter	1 t. salt
4 T. flour	Dash nutmeg
2 C. milk	¼ t. pepper

Saute onion and garlic with 2 tsp. butter until soft. Add meat. Cook, stirring with fork to break up meat. Add tomatoes, bay leaf, salt and pepper. Simmer, covered, for around 45 minutes.

Either fry or boil potatoes. (slice thinly first, of course). They should be almost done. Now arrange layers of potatoes, meat and tomato mixture in casserole finishing with layer of potatoes.

Now make your sauce! Melt better over low heat; add flour, salt, pepper and nutmeg – stir until well blended. Remove from heat. Very gradually stir in milk and return to heat. Cook, stirring constantly, until thick and smooth. Now, place a bit of this sauce in a bowl and gradually stir in two eggs which you have beaten beforehand. While stirring big pot of sauce, add this mixture into it. Stir and DO NOT overheat.

Pour this sauce over your mousaka. Bake uncovered in 350 degree oven for 35 to 45 minutes. Will be golden brown. Let sit a few minutes before cutting. Will come out in perfect squares if you do this correctly.

SPANAKOPITTA (SPINACH PIE)

1 Pkg, phyllo (filo)	5 Eggs, beaten well
Mixture corn oil and butter	¾ lb. Feta cheese, crumbled
4 Pkg. frozen chopped spinach	Chopped parsley and dill weed
Bunch green onions, chopped finely	Pepper
1 T. uncooked rice	1/3 C. butter, melted

Cook the spinach and drain, running cold water over it until it can be handled. Now squeeze every bit of moisture out of it that you can (use small bunches). Add olive oil, onion, Feta, eggs, dill weed and pepper.

BUtter an oblong pan (large type) and place 1 sheet of filo on it. Brush liberally with mixture of corn oil and butter. Add 6 more sheets in the same manner, buttering each well – let them come up to the sides of the pan. Spread spinach filling over entire thing evenly. Cover with 6 more sheets of filo. Brush tops with corn oil-butter mixture. Sprinkle the top with water to prevent curling. Trim around sides with knife.

Bake for 45 minutes or so (should be golden brown) at 350. Cool slightly, cut into squares and serve. You can serve this hot or cold, although I prefer it hot.

PASTICCIO

1 lb. elbow macaroni

For Sauce

½ C. butter
1 Lb. chopped (ground) round beef   Nutmeg
½ C. butter   Cinnamon
1 C. chopped onions   Cloves
1- I Lb. can tomatoes or   3 Egg whites
2 T. tomato paste (instructor preferred this)   1 C. Italian bread crumbs
1 Small glass white wine   1 C.Kefalotiri cheese, specialty
Parsley and oregano to taste   shop item.
Greek cheese   Parsley, oregano

White Sauce:

4 C. milk
3 Egg yolks
1 C Parmesan cheese
1/3 C. flour
1 t. salt
3 T. butter
½ t. each nutmeg, cinnamon, cloves

This is a bit tricky and requires concentration, but the results are superb. This recipe makes enough to serve even 10 people pretty comfortably. If you do this correctly, you will be able to cut it in perfect squares.

First, prepare your meat sauce with ingredients listed above under "Sauce". Once it is cooked, cover and reduce to simmer. Once it is quite cooled down, add ½ cup of the Italian bread crumbs and stir gently.
Now boil your macaroni being careful not to overcook. Drain, place in a sauce-pan. Add ½ cup butter and stir. Then stir in 3 unbeaten egg whites and 1 cup of Kefalotiri cheese.

Butter a very large baking dish (9x13 at least) and sprinkle the bottom with ½ cup dried bread crumbs. Add enough of the macaroni mixture to cover the bottom dish. Now cover with part of the meat sauce. Continue this, ending more or less with macaroni on top. Time to make the "White Sauce", making the usual white sauce over low heat first, (milk, flour, salt, butter, nutmeg). Let sauce cool briefly – take some out and gently stir in 3 unbeaten egg yolks, ½ cup of Parmesan.

Gently pour the white sauce over your pasticcio mixture, being sure that you cover it thoroughly so that it seeps down into all parts and as well as the corners. Do this slowly to insure success. Sprinkle the remaining cheese and bread crumbs over it. Melt some butter, ½ cup or so and pour over the entire pasticcio. This mixture of remaining cheese, melted butter and bread crumbs will form a lovely crust.

Bake this in a 400 degree oven until golden brown, about 40 to 45 minutes should suffice.

If you remove this dish too soon, the egg will not have hardened and you will have a sloppy, but tasty mess. If you remove it too late, it will be somewhat singed. If the top seems alarmingly brown before the 40 to 45 minute time, cover it with aluminum foil or reduce heat a little. The high heat is required to produce a good product.

Sweets

LEMON STACK PIE

Picked this recipe up at a quilting class I took. We potlucked it for lunch and this was one of the dessert offerings. It is luscious!

1 – 9 Inch double pie crust (recipe of your choice)
2 t. unflavored gelatin
1/3 C. fresh lemon juice
1 ½ C. sugar
1 ½ T. butter or margarine
1 T. lemon zest
3 Large eggs, beaten
1 C. whipping cream, whipped

Using half of pie crust dough, line pie plate and bake for 8 minutes at 475 degrees. From remaining dough cut 2- 6 ½ inch circles. Prick and bake for 8 minutes for 475 degrees.

Sprinkle gelatin over lemon juice in a small saucepan. Let stand 1 minute. Add sugar, butter and lemon zest. Cook, stirring constantly over medium-low heat until gelatin dissolves.

Gradually stir ¼ of the hot mixture into the beaten eggs; pour back into remaining hot mixture, stirring constantly. Cook over low heat continuing to stir constantly for 13 minutes. Cover and chill until consistency of unbeaten egg white. Fold half of the whipped cream into lemon mixture.

Spoon 1/3 of lemon mixture into prepared pastry shell. Top with l of the baked pastry circles. Repeat layers ending with lemon mixture. Cover with wax paper and chill.

PEANUT BUTTER AND FUDGE SWIRL PIE

This is a Mary Margrave dessert making. . . .   Yummy

1 Pkg. (8 oz.) Philadelphia Cream Cheese, softened
½ C. sugar
½ C. creamy peanut butter
2 C. thawed Cool Whip Whipped Topping
1 Oreo pie crust (6 oz.)
¼ C. Hot Fudge Ice Cream Topping

Beat Cream Cheese, sugar and peanut butter in large bowl with mixer in blender.
Gently fold in 2 C. of Cool Whip.

Spoon into crust, drizzle with fudge topping. Swirl gently with a knife..
Refrigerate 4 hours or until firm. Refrigerate leftovers.
Special extras: Sprinkle with chopped Planters Cocktail peanuts or Hershey's
Chocolate (shaved). Serve.

PEANUT BUTTER PIE

Feeling as though I were lost in time, I made a trip to Shipshewana, Indiana for a day one beautiful summer and experienced the real food serving the Amish do when they are in barn raisings or once a month church services. I discovered peanut butter pie which sent me to the moon. I also discovered a peaceful group of people who live the very simple life void of material glitter and continue to live plainly. I found that I too could design and make quilts (with an electric sewing machine) and make their humble food recipes (with a gas stove). I was so impressed with their peaceful way of life that in one Lent I read 16 of their books. I am in bewildered awe. I will however offer you this pie recipe which is one of their prides (Pride is not one of their attributes, however).

Crumbs:
>   2/3 C. confectioner's sugar
>   1/3 C. crunchy peanut butter

Mix together until fine crumbs are formed. Sprinkle half of crumb mix in bottom of baked pie shell. Reserve other half of crumbs for topping.

Filling:
>   2 Egg yolks, beaten
>   1/3 C. sugar
>   1 T. flour
>   1 T. cornstarch
>   2 C. milk
>   1 T. butter
>   1 t. vanilla
>   1 9-inch pie shell

Combine sugar, flour, and cornstarch. Add to beaten egg yolks. Mix to form a smooth paste. Add milk and cook, stirring constantly until thickened. Remove from heat and stir in butter and vanilla.

Pour partly cooled filling into baked pie shell. When cooled, sprinkle with remaining crumb mixture. Serve with whipped cream.

SWEET POTATO PIE

Crust:
18 Graham crackers (2 ½" squares)
1 ½ oz. cereal nuggets
2 T. Apple cider
1 Lightly beaten egg white
2 t. vegetable or walnut oil
½ t. almond extract

Filling:
1 Lb. sweet potatoes, baked until very soft and peeled
1 C. evaporated milk
½ C. egg, whipped
½ C. apple cider
¼ C.+ 2 T. firmly packed brown sugar
1 t. vanilla extract
¾ t. cinnamon
¾ t. ground ginger
¼ t. ground cloves

1) To prepare crust, spray 9" pie pan with nonstick cooking spray.
2) In food processor or blender, process graham crackers until finely crumbled. In medium bowl, add cereal and sugar to cracker crumbs; Blend with fork. Add cider, egg white, oil and almond extract; blend with fork until completely moistened. Press crumb mixture evenly onto bottom and sides of prepared pan; cover with plastic wrap and chill at least 10 minutes.
3) To prepare filling, set oven rack in lower 1/3 of oven and preheat to 375°
4) In food processor or blender, or with electric mixer on medium speed, blend sweet potatoes and milk until smooth. Add remaining ingredients and process just until blended (do not over beat). Pour into prepared pie shell.
5) Bake 40 – 50 minutes or until a knife inserted to center comes out clean.

Cool on wire rack to room temperature; cut into 8 wedges and serve.

AUNTIE GREET'S PIE CRUST

4 C. flour
1 Lb. lard

In a measuring cup, beat 1 egg and 1 tsp. vinegar. Fill cup with milk and put together with dry ingredients and lard. Incorporate. Roll out and bake at 350 degrees.

LEMONADE PIE

Given to me by one of my students who loved to cook and stir as much as I did.

2 – 9 oz. Cool Whip
2 Small cans lemonade concentrate
2 Cans of Eagle brand sweetened condensed milk
Yellow food coloring
3 – 9 Inch graham cracker pie crusts

Whip together, pour into pie crusts.

CHERRIES IN THE SNOW

2 ½ C. graham cracker crumbs
½ Lb. melted butter
8 Oz. pkg. cream cheese

2 C. sifted powdered sugar
2 t. vanilla
½ Pt. whipped cream
2 Cans of Thank You brand cherries

Mix together graham cracker crumbs and melted butter. Line 9x13" cake pan and bake at 350 degrees for 7 min. Cool. Mix together cream cheese and 2 C. sifted powdered sugar. Add 2 t. vanilla to whipped cream. Fold into cheese mixture. Put in crust. Refrigerate. Just before serving pour 2 cans of "Thank You" brand cherries over the mixture.

REAL SOUTHERN PECAN PIE

After lemon meringue, pecan pie is my very favorite. Here is one that will knock your socks off.

½ Stick of butter, melted
1 C. brown sugar
½ C. white sugar
2 T. milk (evaporated or cream)
Handful of pecan nuts for the top

1 t. vanilla
Pinch of salt
1 T. flour
2 or 3 Eggs (2 large or 3 small)

Mix all ingredients but nuts. Add nuts, pour in unbaked shell. Bake 45 min. at 400 degrees

MINCEMEAT PIE

You either love it or hate it. My dad loved this pie and I have made it every Thanksgiving since his passing in 1975. I do not make the old fashioned pie with meat; I found a recipe that was good, easy and delicious (if you like mincemeat pie. . . .and I do). This came from the pages of the now defunct Gourmet magazine which touted really good food fare. I lost the recipe in a move from Portland, OR to Kalamazoo, Michigan, called the national award winning Kalamazoo Public Library and they found it, copied it for me and so I share it with you.

Filling:

5 Granny Smith apples, peeled, and chopped
1 C dark raisins
1 C. golden raisins
½ C. chopped mixed candied citrus peels
1 t. freshly grated lemon zest
1 ¼ C. firmly packed dark brown sugar
2 T. unsalted butter
1 T. cider vinegar
½ t. salt
1 ½ t. cinnamon
1 t. ground allspice
¼ t. freshly grated nutmeg   (Continued on next page)

¼ t. freshly ground black pepper
¼ C. dark rum

Make the filling: In a kettle combine the apples, raisins, the candied peels, the zest, brown sugar, butter, the vinegar, salt, the cinnamon, the allspice, the nutmeg, the pepper, and 1 ½ c. water, bring the mixture to a boil, stirring and let simmer, stirring occasionally, for 40 minutes, or until the liquid is very thick. Add the rum and simmer the mixture, stirring for 10 minutes, or until the liquid is almost evaporated. Let the filling cool, transfer it to an airtight container, and chill for 1 day to allow the flavors to develop. The filling may be made 1 week in advance and kept chilled. I use a good store bought pie dough (enough for a double crusted one). Throw the filling into the 9-inch pie pan you have prepared, covered it with the second pie round, and make steamer slits. Be sure that your edges are well sealed. Bake in a 400 degree oven for ½ hour and then on 350 degrees for another ½ hour. It should be bubbly and golden brown.

In case you haven't noticed, very good dishes show up in abundance during some time periods. Here is one that popped up during the 1960s and everyone simply had to make it.

GRASSHOPPER PIE

16 Oreo cookies
3 T. Melted butter
¾ C. milk
2 T. crème de menthe

1 T. crème de cocoa
30 Large marshmallows
½ Pt. whipping cream

Throw the cookies in a large plastic storage bag and use a rolling pin to crush them. In a large bowl, dump the cookies in and add the melted butter and mix. Pat into a 9 inch pie plate saving a few crumbs for the top. Place milk and marshmallows in a double boiler. When this recipe was developed, microwave ovens were not in existence so you could carefully melt this duo in there also. Keep a close eye on the melting process as you continue to stir until smooth. Add whipped cream and liqueurs. Pour into crust; top with crumbs and refrigerate overnight.

TURTLE PUMPKIN PIE

1/3 C. plus 2 Tbsp. caramel topping, divided
1 Graham cracker pie crust
½ C. plus 2 Tbsp. pecan pieces, divided
1 C. cold milk
2 Pkgs. (4-serving size each) Jell-O vanilla flavor Instant Pudding/Pie filling
1 C. canned pumpkin
1 t. ground cinnamon
½ t. ground nutmeg
1 Tub (8oz.) Cool Whip whipped topping thawed, divided Pour: ¼ C. caramel topping onto crust, sprinkle with ½ pecans.

Beat: milk, dry pudding mixes, pumpkin and spices with whisk until blended. Stir in 1 ½ cups whipped topping. Spread onto crust. Top with remaining whipped topping.

Refrigerate 1 hour. Top with pecans and drizzle remaining caramel with fork. Store leftovers in refrigerator. Makes 10 servings

EASY LEMON SQUARES

I had a wonderful neighbor in my early years of homemaking by the name of Claire Belfer. She and her husband, Harvey, would have my sons and me over for Hanukah each year they lived across the street from us. I associate a lot of things she cooked as Claire's Jewish food. She was a superlative cook and we still connect once a year, she from West Palm Beach and me from Kalamazoo and rattle on about philosophy.

Base:
1 Pkg. lemon pudding including yellow cake mix
2 C. crushed corn flakes cereal
1/2 C. firmly packed brown sugar
1/3 C. chopped nuts
½ C. butter, softened

Filling:
3 oz. package lemon pudding/pie filling (not instant)
14 oz. can sweetened condensed milk (not evaporated)
¾ t. lemon extract

Glaze:
1 C. powdered sugar, sifted; ¼ t. lemon extract; 3-5 t. water

FROZEN LEMONADE SQUARES

18 Squares Low Fat Honey Grahams, finely crushed (about 1-1/4 cups crumbs)
1/3 C. butter, melted
1 Qt. frozen vanilla yogurt, softened
1 Can (6 oz.) frozen lemonade concentrate, thawed
½ C. thawed Cool Whip Lite Whipped Topping
Mint springs and lemon slices (optional)

1. Mix crumbs and butter. Press firmly onto bottom of 9-inch square pan.
2. Beat yogurt and lemonade concentrate in large bowl with electric mixer on medium speed until well blended. Spread over crust.
3. Freeze 4 hours or until firm. Cut into squares. Serve each square topped with a dollop of whipped topping, mint sprigs and lemon slices, if desired.

CREAM PUFF SHELLS

Preheat oven to 400 degrees
Have eggs at room temperature (which means take them out the night before).
It is best to have high gluten flour. Sift before measuring.

1 C. high gluten flour or all purpose flour
1/8 t. salt
1 T. sugar, if puffs are to be used with sweet filling

Place in a heavy pan: 1 cup water or milk and 1/8 cup butter
When mixture boils, add flour in one fell swoop and stir quickly with a wooden spoon. It looks rough at first, but suddenly becomes smooth, at which point you stir faster. In a few minutes the paste becomes dry, does not cling to the spoon or the sides of the pan and when the spoon is pressed on it lightly, it leaves a smooth imprint.

Do not overcook for then the dough will fail to puff. Remove pan from heat for about 2 minutes. It never returns to the heat and this is why, to cook properly, the eggs must be at room temperature. Add one at a time beating vigorously after each addition, 4 to 5 eggs.

Continue to beat each time until the dough no longer looks slippery. The paste is ready bake when the last egg has been incorporated, and it has reached proper consistency when a small quantity of the dough will stand erect if scooped up on the end of the spoon.

It is best to use the dough at once. Use another spoon to plop the dough onto a parchment lined baking pan and allow for expansion (do not crowd them). Sprinkle a few drops of water over them lightly as you would sprinkle laundry. Place in the 400 degree oven for 10 minutes. Reduce the heat to 350 degrees and bake for about 25 minutes longer. Do not remove them from the oven until they are quite firm to the touch. Cool shells away from any draft before filling them. For filling, cut them horizontally with a sharp knife. If there are any damp dough filaments inside, be sure to remove them.

(continued on next page)

FILLING FOR CREAM PUFFS

2 C. milk
1 8 oz. pkg. cream cheese
1- 3 ¾ -oz. pkg. instant vanilla pudding mix
8 Cream puffs (see recipe above)
Caramel topping

Gradually add ½ cup milk to softened cream cheese, mixing until well blended. Add pudding mix and remaining milk; beat slowly 1 minute. Cover surface of pudding with waxed paper or transparent wrap. Chill. Cut tops from cream puffs; fill with pudding mixture. Replace tops and spoon topping over. 8 servings

KELLOGG'S ORIGINAL RICE KRISPIES TREATS

When I was very young, WW II was raging and marshmallows were not to be had because sugar was rationed. I was not privy to Treats but as a mother who was a feminist and bound to make sure that she could do it all, I would make these wonderful desserts for my sons. Now they are commercially made and moms and dads simply buy them but I noticed that my son, Jarl, still made them for his brood of 4. So I offer this simple recipe to be enjoyed by newer generations and so do!

3 T. butter or margarine
1 Package (10 oz. about 40) regular marshmallows,
    or 4 C. miniature marshmallows
6 C. Rice Krispies cereal

1. In a large sauce pan melt butter over low heat. Add marshmallows and stir until completely melted. Remove from heat.
2. Add Rice Krispies cereal and stir until well coated.
3. Using a butter coated spatula or waxed paper evenly press into a 13 x 9 inch pan coated with cooking spray. Cool. Cut into 2 inch squares. Best if served the same day.

You may use a microwave oven melting the butter and marshmallows in a large microwave safe bowl then following the above directions.

MICROWAVE CARMEL CORN

3 Qt. popped corn
1 C. dark brown sugar
¼ C. white corn syrup
1 stick margarine
½ t. soda(

Combine sugar, corn syrup and margarine in 4 cup glass measure. Bring to a boil in microwave oven (full power) 2 to 4 minutes. Stir in soda. Spray a large paper grocery bag with Pam or the likes. Pour hot mixture into bag over popped corn, shake. Close bag and cook on full power 1 minutes 30 seconds. Shake. Cook 1 minute 30 seconds. Shake. Cook 30 seconds. Shake. Cook 30 seconds. Pour onto jelly roll pan.

Doubling this recipe and baking in large cake tin serves 15

PARTY SPONGE CAKE

June O'Connell was the mother to four very bright boys. How she managed I do not know. She cooked and stirred and taught school! This is one of her recipes and I lay it out to you because I was friends with her two eldest sons, Joe and Charlie.

Make your favorite sponge cake. Slice through twice and spread sweetened whpped cream between layers. Let stand in refrigerator over night, - - - several days is all right. Cover with whipped cream when ready to serve.

CREAM ALMOND FILLING
(FOR ANGEL FOOD CAKE)

Cook in double boiler until thick: ½ pt. sweet cream
3 beaten egg yolks
1 t. cornstarch
1 rounded T. sugar

Flavor (almond, vanilla or lemon extract etc.). Add toasted slivered almonds. Put between angel food cake layers and serve with whipped cream topping.

WILLIE HEINIG'S DECADENTLY DELICIOUS CAKE

When I first moved to Kalamazoo, Michigan I lived in an apartment at a lovely place called Parkview Hills. To get acquainted with some of people of the Zoo, I did hand work, knitting, cross stitching and needlepoint with a large group of ladies whose ages rallied somewhere around 80; I was in my early sixties. I learned a lot from these old women who had lived interesting lives, shared patterns as well as recipes. This one came from one of my favorite ladies who had fabulous recipes and I wish that I had her recipe book.

1 pkg. yellow cake mix
1 11 oz-can of mandarin oranges + its juice
4 eggs
½ C. oil

Beat the above together and pour into a greased 9x 13 cake pan. Bake at 350 degrees for 25- 30 minutes. Cool completely.

(continued on next page)

FROSTING

1 8 oz. container of Cool Whip
1 20 oz. can crushed pineapple + juice
1 3 ½ oz. pkg. instant vanilla pudding mix

Carefully mix the above together and frost the cooled cake. Store in refrigerator.

KRIS LIEBERT'S COCONUT MILK CAKE

High School student, Kris, came into my office one day with a cake, a marvelous cake and asked if she please could be switched to my end of the alphabet (M-Z). Henceforth, she became Kris Tiebert as did her adorable brother, Adam who ended up a wonder at WMU, playing violin in Western's orchestra. Subsequently, he now plays with both the Kalamazoo Symphony and the Grand Rapids Symphony – I am so very proud of both of these kids though I haven't seen either of them in years. I do have this fabulous recipe to remember them by and I offer it to you.

Preheat oven to 350.
Have all ingredients at about 75 degrees (I am going to say room temp.)
Have ready:
>1 ½ C. freshly grated coconut
>Sift before measuring: 3 C. cake flour
>Resift it with:
>3 t. double acting baking powder
>½ t. salt
>Sift: 1 ½ C. sugar
>Cream well: ¾ C. butter

Add the sifted sugar gradually and continue creaming until these ingredients are very light, Beat in: 3 beaten egg yolks, add the sifted flour mixture in 3 parts to the butter mixture, alternately with: ¾ cup coconut milk or milk and ½ t. vanilla. Stir the batter until smooth after each addition. Then add ¾ cup of grated coconut. Whip until stiff, but not dry: 3 egg whites

Fold the egg whites gently into the batter. Bake in greased layer pans for about 25 minutes. To serve, fill between the layers with: currant, strawberry or raspberry jelly. Cover the cake with: Seven minutes white icing, coat with the remaining ¾ cup grated coconut. (see next page)

Seven Minute White Icing (this frosts the coconut cake)

Place in the top of a double boiler and beat until thoroughly blended:

2 unbeaten egg whites
1 ½ C. sugar
5 T. cold water
¼ t. cream of tarter
1 ½ t. light corn syrup

Place these ingredients over rapidly boiling water and beat them constantly with a rotary beater or whisk for 7 minutes. Remove icing from heat and add:
1 t. vanilla

Continue beating until icing is the right consistency to frost cake. You may add to it at this point i.e. ½ cup nuts, chopped, grated coconut or berries.

SHEATH CAKE & FROSTING

I am not sure where Jane Ewing, Sowle, Gordon, Maksymouwski got her terrific recipes, but they were always new and different. This is hers.

1 stick margarine
3 T, cocoa
½ C. shortening
1 C. water
2 C. flour
2 C. sugar

2 eggs
1 t. vanilla
½ C. buttermilk
1 t. soda
1 t. cinnamon

Frosting 1:
1 stick margarine
2 T. cocoa
6 T. milk

1 box powdered sugar
1 C. pecans, chopped
1 t. vanilla

Mix first four ingredients together in a saucepan. Melt, bring to a boil and pour over flour and sugar. Mix well and add eggs, vanilla, buttermilk, soda and cinnamon. Mix well (batter sill be very thin). Bake in a 400-degree oven for 25 minutes in a greased and floured 11 x 14 inch pan. (continued on next page)

Frosting 2:
Start 5 minutes before cake is to come out of oven. Bring to a boil margarine, cocoa, and milk. Then add powdered sugar, pecans, and vanilla. Ice the cake immediately. Let cool and cut into squares to serve.

Beat whipping cream and vanilla until foamy; gradually add powdered sugar, beating until peaks form.

Frosting 3:
1- 6 ounce package semi-sweet
    Chocolate morsels
2 ½ C. powdered sugar, sifted

½ C. half-n-half
¾ C. butter

Combine chocolate morsels, ½ cup half-n-half, and butter in a saucepan; cook over medium heat, stirring until chocolate melts. Remove from heat; add powdered sugar, mixing well.

(continued on next page)

Set saucepan in ice and beat until frosting holds its shape and loses its gloss. Add a few more drops of half-n-half, if needed. Spread filling between layers and spread frosting over top and sides of cake.

Refrigerate until ready to serve.

SUZI MITTELSTEADT'S MOTHER'S CHOCOLATE CHIP CAKE

Suzi is one of my dearest friends whom I met in a quilting class some 16 years ago when I first moved from Oregon to Michigan. She and her husband, Tom, had left Florida so we both were new to the area. We can talk for hours: books, quilting, philosophy, politics and health. I am so grateful to have this recipe from her who is the quintessential Chocolate eater and Tom brings her chocolates we would all die for.

1 C. sugar
¾ C. shortening (Crisco)
1 ¼ C. plus 2 T. flour
2 beaten eggs
1 ½ T. cocoa
1 C. dates
1 ¼ C. boiling water over dates w/1 t. soda added, ¼ tsp salt.
½ c. walnuts

Cut dates; pour boiling water over and add soda. Mix sugar and shortening; add beaten eggs. Alternate flour with date mixture. Put in pan (9x13) . Over top sprinkle 16 oz. pkg. chocolate chips and ½ c. of walnuts. Put over this, ½ c sugar. Bake 25-30 minutes at 340 degrees.

PERFECT CHOCOLATE CAKE

1 C. cocoa
2 C. boiling water
1 C. butter, softened
2 ½ C. sugar
1 ½ t. vanilla extract

2 ¾ C. flour
2 t, baking soda
½ t. baking powder
½ t, salt
4 eggs

Combine cocoa and boiling water, stirring until smooth, set aside to cool. Combine butter, sugar, eggs, and vanilla, beat until light and fluffy (about 5 minutes).

Combine dry ingredients; add to sugar mixture alternately with cocoa mixture; beginning and ending with flour mixture. Do not over beat! Pour batter into 3 greased and floured 9-inch round cake pans.

Bake at 350 degrees for 25 to 30 minutes or until toothpick comes out of the center clean. Cool in pans for 10 minutes; remove and cool completely.

Filling:

1 cup whipping cream
¼ cup powdered sugar

1 teaspoon vanilla extract

Beat whipping cream and vanilla until foamy; gradually add powdered sugar, beating until peaks form.

Frosting:

1- 6 ounce package semi-sweet
    Chocolate morsels
2 ½ cups powdered sugar, sifted

½ cup half-n-half
¾ cup butter

Combine chocolate morsels, ½ cup half-n-half, and butter in a saucepan; cook over medium heat, stirring until chocolate melts. Remove from heat; add powdered sugar, mixing well.

Set saucepan in ice and beat until frosting holds its shape and loses its gloss. Add a few more drops of half-n-half, if needed. Spread filling between layers and spread frosting over top and sides of cake.

Refrigerate until ready to serve.

ITALIAN CREAM CAKE

1 stick butter
½ C. Crisco (butter flavored)
2 C. sugar
5 egg yolks
2 C. flour

1 C. buttermilk
1 t. soda
1 t. vanilla
1 C. coconut
1 C. pecans, chopped
5 egg whites

Cream together butter, Crisco, sugar, and egg yolks. Mix and add to creamed mixture, flour, buttermilk, soda, vanilla, coconut and pecans. (Note: I add 1 teaspoon of soda to 1 cup buttermilk and give it time to work; then stir it. Alternate flour and buttermilk to the creamed mixture.)

Add 5 egg whites that have been beaten stiff and fold these in last. Bake at 3340 degrees for 30 minutes in three 9-inch greased and floured round cake pans. (This makes a LARGE cake!)

Icing:

1-8 ounce package cream cheese
1 stick butter

1 t. vanilla
1 box powdered sugar

Cream cheese, softened butter, and vanilla together. Beat in powdered sugar to form icing. Ice cake between layers, on top and on sides after cake has cooled

RUSK CAKE

Pat Woodrick was the holder of many wonderful recipes. She was the wife of Dick and mother to 4 children and yet found time to help her community out, play bridge and cook up a storm. This was one of my favorites of Pat's holdings.

6 eggs
1 C. sugar
1 C. ground Rusk
½ C. nut meats
1 t. baking powder

Frosting:
½ pt. whipping cream
½ C. powdered sugar
½ C. milk
4 packages Milk Duds

Cream together 6 egg yolks and the sugar, Combine with the ground Rusk, chopped nut meats, baking powder and vanilla. Beat the egg whites and fold into mixture. Put in 13 x 9 inch greased pan and bake at 350 degrees for 30 minutes.

Cool cake.

Beat the whipping cream and spread on cake. Place in refrigerator. Melt the Milk Duds and remove from heat and cool. Drizzle over whipping cream and place back in refrigerator. About 3 hours before serving, cover cake with foil. Very moist and good.

BETTER THAN ALMOST ANYTHING CAKE

This recipe came from Peggy, a great lady who belonged to the same knitting group I attended. Everyone requested that she bring this cake to our Friday night lock-ins which she did and we would all applaud when it was served. Easy, moist and wonderfully tasting.

1 package Betty Crocker Super Moist German chocolate cake mix
Water, vegetable oil and eggs as called for on the package directions
1 can (14oz.) sweetened condensed milk
1 jar (16-17 oz.) caramel, butterscotch or fudge topping
1 container (8 oz.) frozen whipped topping, thawed
1 bag (8 oz.) toffee chips or bits

Heat oven to 350 degrees.

Make and bake cake as directed on package for 13 x 9 pan. Cool 15 minutes. Punch a hole in the top of the warm cake every 1//2 inch with the handle of a wooden spoon. Drizzle the milk over the top of cake, let stand until it has been absorbed into cake. Drizzle with caramel topping. Run knife around sides of pan to loosen cake. Cover and refrigerate about 2 hours or until chilled. Spread whipped topping over top of cake. Sprinkle with toffee chips. Store covered in refrigerator.

PAULA DEEN'S MOLTEN LAVA CAKE

This recipe can be made ahead and refrigerated for 2 to 3 days. Paula says that it is great alone, but can be topped with ice cream or a raspberry sauce. I have only had it with ice cream. **YUMMO!**

Serves 6

6 1-oz. bittersweet chocolate squares
2 1-oz. semi-sweet chocolate baking squares
10 T. butter
½ C. all purpose flour
1 ½ C. confectioners' sugar
3 large eggs
3 egg yolks
1 t. vanilla extract
2 T. Grand Marnier

1. Preheat oven to 425 degrees. Grease 6 (6 ounce) custard cups
2. Melt chocolates and butter in the microwave or in a double boiler. Add flour and sugar to chocolate mixture. Stir in eggs until smooth. Stir in vanilla and Grand Marnier. Divide batter evenly among custard cups.
3. Bake for 14 minutes. Edges should be firm but the center will be runny. Run Knife around the edge to loosen and invert onto dessert plate.
4. Top with ice cream or raspberry sauce.
5. If you have let the cakes chill, pop them in the microwave just to warm them so the "lava" will run out when spooned into.

5 MINUTE CHOCOLATE MUG CAKE

This is a fun wee thing to make and tastes pretty good too. Cousin Margo sent it to me on the net and I made it.

4 T. flour
4 T. sugar
2 T. cocoa
1 egg
3 T. milk
3 T. oil
3 T. chocolate chips (optional)
A small splash of vanilla extract (I also use almond extract)
1 large coffee mug (MicroSafe)

Add dry ingredients to mug and mix well. Add the egg and mix thoroughly. Pour in milk and oil and mix well. Add the chocolate chips (if using) and extract and mix again. Put your mug in the microwave and cook for 1 ½ to 3 minutes at 1000 watts. The cake will rise over the top of the mug, but don't be alarmed. Allow to cool and then tip out onto a plate. EAT! This can serve 2 if you wish to feel more virtuous. Add whipped cream, ice cream to really feel the guilt rising. And why is this the most dangerous cake recipe in the world? Because now we are only 5 minutes away from chocolate at any time of the

LEMON CREAM CAKE

Melts in your mouth . . . . .

1 16-18 oz. pound cake (already baked)
1 ½ sticks butter (12 Tbs.)
2 C. sugar
4 eggs beaten lightly
4 lemons, juiced – approximately ¾ cup juice
¼ C.finely grated fresh lemon rind
8 oz. whipping cream
1 t. vanilla
1 lemon, sliced for garnish
Plastic wrap

Place pound cake in freezer for ease in handling. When cake is frozen trim brown edges from cake and slice horizontally into four sections. Allow to thaw and wrap in plastic wrap until ready to use.

LEMON SAUCE

Melt butter in top of double boiler; stir in sugar, eggs, lemon juice and rind. Cook over gently boiling water for approximately 18-20 minutes, stirring frequently until sauce thickens. Chill.

Place bottom layer of cake on an extra-large sheet of plastic wrap, cover with at least 1/3 cup of lemon sauce. Repeat with remaining layers. Spread around cake to seal. Chill overnight.

When ready to serve, whip cream with sugar and vanilla added. Place a dollop of whipped cream on each slice of cake and garnish with a lemon slice. Serves 8-10.

Be generous with the lemon filling between layers. Cake will soak up the sauce. This light dessert can be made two to three days ahead. Store extra sauce in refrigerator to use on muffins, lady fingers, or over angel food cake.

ORANGE CAKE

This was a recipe mom confiscated from Mrs. Frank Dubois, wife of the owner of a local grocery. As I have repeatedly said, mom had a real knack for good tasting things.

1 C. sugar
½ C. lard or Crisco
2 eggs
1 C. sour milk
1 t. soda
2 t. baking powder
2 C. sifted bread flour
½ t. salt

Grind together 1 cup of dates, ½ cup of crushed nuts, rind of 1 orange. Bake 350. Dissolve juice of 1 orange in ½ cup sugar and pour over cake while hot.

BANANA CAKE

This recipe is 80 years old (from what I can gather) and came from a friend of my mother's by the name of Mrs. Walter Nord whom I never met.

Cream: 1 ¼ C. sugar
            ½ C. shortening
Add: 1 C. mashed bananas
            2 eggs, beaten
Sift   2 C. flour   - - - - - -Sift 3 times so all three ingredients mix
            2 t. baking powder
            ¼ t. salt
Add: ½ C. boiling water
            ½ C, sour cream
            1 t. baking soda
            1 t. vanilla

Mix well and bake in 2 greased layer tins. Makes a large cake. Bake at 350 til done. For frosting, cream together 4 T. butter with 2 cups powdered sugar and add vanilla

EASY LEMON CAKE

1 pkg. (2-layer size) lemon cake mix
2 pkg. (3.4 oz. size) Jell-o Lemon instant pudding
1 ½ cups cold milk
1 tub (8 oz. size) Cool Whip, thawed

Prepare and bake cake mix according to directions on package for 2 (8 or 9 inch) round cake layers. Cool completely.

Beat Lemon pudding mixes with milk using a whisk for 2 minutes. Immediately spread on cake layers. Stack cake layers and frost with Cool Whip. Top with lemon slices and mint.

LEMON SPONGE CUPS

2 T. butter
1 C. sugar
¼ C. sifted flour
5 T. lemon juice
¼ t. salt
The rind of 1 lemon, grated
3 eggs, separated
1 ½ C. milk

Cream butter. Add sugar, flour and lemon juice. Mix well and add lemon rind, salt and yolks which have been mixed with milk. Fold in beaten egg whites,

Bake in custard cups in pan of water. Bake 350 for 45 minutes. Frost with your own icing.

Ganache

12 oz. chocolate, chopped into small pieces
1 C. heavy cream
Optional 3 T. flavored liqueur

Place chocolate pieces in a large large bowl. Heat heavy cream on medium high until it comes to a boil. Remove from heat and immediately pour cream over chocolate and stir until completely mixed and glossy. Allow ganache to cool before pouring over cakes as a glaze. The longer you allow the ganache to cool, the thicker it will set. Typically I stick mine in the refrigerator so it is slightly cold before whipping. You might want to use a ladle to generate the pouring of the mixture onto the cake.

ELAINE SELANDER'S 2 EGG CAKE

Another of the Swedish lady's delights. . . . .

2 ¼ C. sifted cake flour
3 ½ t. baking powder
1 t. salt
1 ½ C. sugar
1 C. milk
1 t. vanilla
½ C. soft shortening
2 large eggs

Sift dry ingredients in a bowl. Add vanilla to milk. Add shortening and 2/3 cup of milk to dry ingredients, beat 2 minutes by clock. Add remaining milk, eggs and beat 2 minutes longer.

Bake in moderate oven (350 degrees) 30 – 40 minutes in two 9-inch pans or an oblong pan 8 x 12 x 2.

MARY MARGRAVE'S MOTHER'S
4 LAYER DELIGHT (CHOCOLATE)

1 C. flour
½ C. chopped pecans
1 stick butter
1 8 oz. block cream cheese
1 C. powdered sugar
1 C. Cool Whip
3 C. milk
2 pkg. Instant Chocolate Pudding
Hershey Bar

1) 1st Layer:
    Slice butter in 9x13 glass pan and melt.
    Mix flour and butter and chopped pecans and press down to make crust
    Bake 15 minutes at 375. Cool

2) 2nd Layer
    Soften 1 – 8 oz. cream cheese
    Mix the powdered sugar (1 cup) and cream cheese together.
    Fold in 1 Cool Whip and spread on cooled crust.

3) 3rd Layer
    Beat milk and chocolate pudding until thick.
    Pour over cream cheese mixture and chill for about 1 hour.

4) 4th Layer
    Top with Cool Whip and Shaved chocolate bar.
    Refrigerate at least 2 hours before serving.

Serves 12

CHOCOLATE-AMARETTO CHEESE CAKE

This was once a top winner for healthy foods. Serve it with your favorite fresh berries/ * I believe this is another contribution from Debra Hiss Brey.

Six 2½-inch graham cracker squares, made into crumbs
2 1/3 C. part-skim ricotta cheese
4 oz. nonfat cream cheese
½ C. sugar
¼ C. unsweetened cocoa powder
1 egg
3 T. all-purpose flour
2 T. Amaretto liqueur
1 t. vanilla extract
2 T. semisweet chocolate chips

*If berries aren't readily available, she garnishes w/Smuckers Light Sugar Free Red Raspberry preserves and a dollop of Cool Whip Light.

1) Preheat the oven to 300°. Spray an 8" spring form pan with nonstick cooking spray. Sprinkle the cracker crumbs evenly over the bottom of the pan.

2) In a blender or food processor, puree the ricotta and cream cheese, the sugar, cocoa, egg, flour, liqueur and vanilla; stir in the chocolate chips.

3) Pour the cheese mixture over the crumbs. Bake until a knife inserted in the center comes out clean, about 1 ½ hours. Cool completely on a rack. Refrigerate, covered, until chilled, at least 3 hours.

CHEESE CAKE SUPREME

My mother worked with a woman named Jeannie Gust who had phenomenal recipes. You know what my mother did with the recipes she collected. Yup, I have every one of them.

3 C. cookie crumbs
½ C. butter

Mix these two items well and pat in a spring form pan.

Mix thoroughly these items and place on top of crumb mixture.

5- 8 oz. pkg. cream cheese
1 ¾ C. sugar
¼ C. whipping cream
3 T. flour
1 T. lemon juice
5 eggs

Bake at 450° for 10 minutes, then 200° for 1 ½ to 2 hours. Cool.

Top with fruit and whipped cream.

PUMPKIN CHEESECAKE

I have taken this treat a few times as my contribution at Thanksgiving instead of pie.

Crust:
1 ½ C. graham cracker crumbs
¼ C. granulated sugar
1/3 C. melted butter

Cheesecake:
3 pkgs. (8 oz. ea.) cream cheese, softened
1 C. granulated sugar
¼ C. packed light brown sugar
1 ¾ C. Libby's Solid Pack Pumpkin
2 eggs
2/3 C. (5-fluid oz. can) undiluted Carnation evaporated milk
2 T. cornstarch
1 ¼ t. ground cinnamon
½ t. ground nutmeg

Topping:
2 C. (16 oz. carton) sour cream, at room temperature
¼ C. to 1/3 cup granulated sugar
1 t. vanilla extract

For Crust: Combine graham cracker crumbs, sugar and melted butter in a medium bowl. Press this mixture onto bottom and 1 inch up side of 9-inch springform pan. Bake in preheated 350 degrees oven for 6 to 8 minutes.. So not allow to brown. Remove from oven and cool.

For Cheesecake: Beat cream cheese, granulated sugar and light brown sugar in a large mixer bowl until light and fluffy. Beat in pumpkin, eggs and evaporated milk. Add corn starch, cinnamon and nutmeg and beat well. Pour into crust. Bake in preheated 350° oven for 55 – 60 minutes or until edge is set.
     6

DAFFODILL CAKE

When I moved to Kalamazoo, Michigan from Portland Oregon I was directed to a marvelous bakery called Mackenzie's. Each Easter time they baked an awesome cake that everyone lusted for. . . it was only baked two or three weeks as a way to celebrate. . . . . it is light and airy.. . . . I have the recipe and here it is to share.

You will need a 9 inch tube pan UNGREASED

1 yellow and white marble cake. Preheat oven to 350 degrees

Sift before measuring:
     1 ½ C. cake flour
     Resift it twice.
     Sift separately 1 ¼ cups sugar

Whip in a glass bowl until frothy:
     10 egg whites
Add: 1 ½ t. salt
     1 t. cream of tartar (makes the whites stand in peaks)
Whip until they hold a point. Fold the sifted sugar in gradually. Separate the mixture into two parts. Fold into one half a little at a time ¾ of the sifted flour and add:
     6 beaten egg yolks
     Grated rind of one orange

Fold into other half, a little at a time
     1/2 C. of sifted flour and
     1 t. vanilla

Place the batters, a cupful or more at a time in the ungreased tub pan. alternating the colors. Bake 45 minutes or until done. Cool by inverting the pan over a bottle. Remove when cool and frost with a good rich butter frosting.

SCHAUM TORTE

6 egg whites
2 C. (scant) sugar
1 T. vinegar
1 t. vanilla
Whipped cream sweetened and flavored with vanilla to taste

Beat egg whites stiff; add sugar, vinegar and vanilla. Beat again until very stiff; fold into ungreased spring mold. Bake at 400 degrees for 3 minutes. Reduce heat to 200 degrees and bake for 7 minutes.

Turn off heat; leave torte in oven for 1 hour without opening the door. Turn out of mold when cold. Cover with whipped cream; serve with crushed fruit.

CHERRY NUT LOAF

1 ½ C. sugar
4 oz. butter
3 eggs separated
2 ½ C. flour
2 t. baking powder
¼ t. salt
¾ C. milk
½ C. chopped walnuts
½ to ¾ C. chopped maraschino cherries or glace cherries, halved

Separate eggs. Beat whites until stiff and set aside. Mix in large bowl, in order given, all ingredients alternating milk and sifted dry ingredients. Fold in egg whites last, pour batter into 9x5 greased loaf pan or 2 or 3 rounds cans. Bake at 350 degrees for 50-55 minutes.

HELLMANN'S CHOCOLATE SENSATION

1 package chocolate cake mix (with pudding in the mix)
1C. Hellmann's Real Mayonnaise
1 C. water
3 eggs

Grease and flour two 9-inch layer cake pans. In large bowl, with mixer at low speed, blend all ingredients 30 seconds. Beat at medium speed 2 minutes or 300 strokes by hand. Pour into prepared pans. Bake in 350 oven 30 to 35 minutes or until cake springs back when touched lightly in center. Cool in pans 10 minutes. Remove: cool on wire racks. Fill and frosts as desired. To prepare cake without pudding in the mix, reduce mayonnaise to ½ cup and increase water to 1 1/3 cups.

APPLE CAKE

2 C. flour
2 t. baking powder
½ C. sugar
2 T. butter/margarine/or shortening
2 eggs
1 C. milk
4 or 5 baking apples, peeled
Sprinkle nutmeg and cinnamon
1 C. sugar
2 T. flour
3 T. butter

Mix first 6 ingredients and pour into 9x 13 greased cake pan. Slice and peel 4 or 5 baking apples, and place on top of batter. Combine 1 cup sugar, 2 tablespoons flour and 3 tablespoons butter, mix together and sprinkle this mixture on top of batter. Then sprinkle cinnamon and nutmeg on top and bake in oven at 325 degrees for one hour.

WHITE CAKE

This is the note that I found on my desk one day at work:
To: Ms. Margrave   From: Bobby Randall
Best recipe! My Great-GrandMother's.
tastes great and is very cheap.

I just loved this kid whom I met him in his freshman year of high school. He looked like the Pillsbury Doughboy and grew into a 6'2" young man by the time he was a senior, having won all sorts of awards for his work in foods. I am sure by now that he is an executive chef somewhere wonderful. Here is the recipe for the cake he wanted me to try.

1st – Boil ½ C. of milk and 1 large T. butter together

2nd – Beat 2 eggs
    1 C. sugar
    1 C. flour
    1 t. baking powder
    1 t. vanilla

Add 1st to 2nd and bake at 325 for 25 – 30 minutes or until edges are golden brown.

Use 1 box of Vanilla (Jiffy) frosting mix

Serves 20
bake in oven at 325 degrees for one hour.

ÉCLAIR BARS

Given to me by Barb Gessner, a good friend and another former secretary. It is so good!

2 pkg. vanilla instant pudding +   3 C. milk   +   9 oz. Cool Whip

Mix pudding with milk. Add Cool Whip. Put layers of graham crackers in bottom of a 9x13 pan. Add ½ of pudding mixture, another layer of graham crackers, remaining pudding mixture and last layer of graham crackers.

Topping: 2 squares of Bakers Chocolate
            3 T. butter
            Melt the above together over hot water
            1 ½ C. powdered sugar (may need more)
            3 T. corn syrup
            3 T. milk
            1 t. vanilla
Blend all and spread on the graham cracker topping.

DATE HORS D'OUERVES

I am a true date lover and so I always looked forward to these little holiday tidbits my mom would make.

1 pound pitted dates
Your choice of nuts: pecans, almonds, walnuts
Granulated sugar

Place nuts in dates and roll in granulated sugar.

BUTTERY PEANUT BRITTLE

Each Christmas my dad would ask for two things, pine soap and peanut brittle, and would receive them. He would have loved this recipe for home made brittle.

2 C. granulated sugar
1 C. light corn syrup
½ C. water
1 C. butter
2 C. peanuts, chopped
1 t. soda
1 candy thermometer

Heat and stir sugar, syrup, and water in 3 qt. sauce pan till sugar dissolves. While syrup boils, blend in butter. Stir often after 230 degrees. Add nuts at 280 degrees. Stir constantly to hard crack stage (305 degrees). Remove from heat.

Quickly stir in soda, mixing well. Pour onto 2 cookie sheets. Stretch thin by lifting and pulling from edges with forks. Loosen from pans as soon as possible. Break up. Makes 2 ½ pounds.

TURTLE CANDY

As a child, my favorite candy (and I received a box each Christmas from Santa) was Turtle Candy. I recently found this recipe. Enjoy!

1 bag Kraft caramels
1 bag chocolate chips
Bag of pecan halves

Warm oven to 200 degrees. Arrange unwrapped caramels on wax paper on baking sheet and place in oven until soft. Melt chocolate chips in microwave. Stir. Flatten caramel into a round with your hands. Press 3 pecan halves into each caramel round so they are peeking out over the edge of the caramel. Replace on baking sheet. When all turtle bases have been made, spread each with chocolate mixture. Refrigerate until cool.

ZUCCHINI SQUARES

Another of daughter-in-law, Debra Hiss Brey's contributions:

2 C. flour
1 t. salt
4 eggs
1 ½ C. sugar
¼ C. brown sugar
2 t. maple syrup
2 t. baking soda
¼ t. baking powder
2 t. t. cinnamon
1 C. vegetable oil
1 C. nuts
2 C, diced zucchini

Combine all ingredients, fold in zucchini last. Spread on greased jelly roll pan. 350 degrees for 30 minutes. Dust w/powdered sugar.

CARMEL CREAMY CANDY

2 C. white sugar
Few grains salt
2 C. cream

2 C. Karo syrup
1 stick butter
1 t.. vanilla

Boil sugar, Karo and salt rapidly to 245 degrees. Add butter and cream gradually so that the mixture does not stop boiling at any time. Cook rapidly to firm ball stage (245 degrees). Stir constantly because the mixture sticks easily at last. Add flavoring and pour into buttered pan (9 x 13); cut into squares and wrap in waxed paper.

MY MAMA'S DATE CAKE

My mother was a labored cook. She didn't seem to take to the culinary arts, but she gave and gave to her community and learned all sorts of new things to share with others. She was always collecting recipes from heaven knows where and passing them on to me . . . this sort of made her a gourmand because she could spot a great dish which of course she wanted me to produce. Whatever the case, this was one of her own crowning glories and I loved this cake from the time I was a little girl when she served it to her bridge club. I got the leftovers, with the whipped cream!!

1 Lb. of pitted dates, cut into small pieces
1 C. boiling water
1 T. butter
1 t. soda
1 Egg, unbeaten
1 C. sugar
1 ¼ C. flour (sift once and measure)

Pour boiling water over the date pieces and let sit for a bit. Mix all ingredients well. Bake in a greased, square pan at 350 degrees, 25 to 30 minutes or until cake leaves side of pan. Serve with whipped cream.

COUSIN MARGO'S CHOCOLATE CRUNCH

One package of chocolate chips
1 large can or bag of Chinese Noodles

Melt chocolate in microwave in a big bowl – stirring until melted.
Add Chinese noodles and mix in chocolate.
Scoop with a teaspoon serving size pieces and place on wax papered pan.
When cool, break away from wax paper and put in candy or serving dish.

DATE TREATS

I used to start with this recipe for the holiday time of Christmas during the month of October and freeze them. I loved them so much; I usually had to make another batch because I would have eaten all of them.

Combine:
1 C. dates, cut up
½ C. sugar
1 egg
¼ lb. melted butter
1 t. vanilla.

Boil for 2 minutes. Add 3 C. Rice Krispies. Cool. Form into balls and roll in crushed nut meats or coconut.

COCONUT MACAROONS

14 ounces sweetened shredded coconut
14 ounces sweetened condensed milk
1 t. pure vanilla extract
2 extra large egg whites at room temperature
¼ t. kosher salt

Preheat oven to 325 degrees.

Combine the coconut, condensed milk, and vanilla in a large bowl. Whip the egg whites and salt with an electric mixer fitted with the whisk attachment until they make medium firm peaks. Carefully fold in the coconut mixture.

Drop the batter onto sheet pans lined with parchment paper using either a 1 ¾ inch diameter ice cream scoop or teaspoons. Bake for 25 to 30 minutes until golden brown.

BAKLAVA

Yes, I did! I made this at Christmas time with great flourish. . . . and thought I was just somethin' else. It's great if you have two of you baking and stirring at the same time but I did not have that luxury. This first time I made this Greek divineness, it took me all afternoon and I couldn't hurry because I was afraid that I would make a mistake. This only mistake I made was not hurrying because I got the Fillo sheet (which at that time I had to find in a specialty store in Grand Rapids) all gummy and gooey from the too wet cloth I had placed on top. So even if you make these once, it's a challenge, a treat and lots of fun.

10 – 15 sheets sheets of Fillo (found in the freezer section of a good market)
2 C. blanched almonds or walnuts or both
1 C. sweet butter
Grind almonds or walnuts, add ½ cup of sugar, cinnamon, and cloves powder to you taste. Combine all ingredients except the Fillo and mix well.

Syrup:
1 C. honey
2 C. of water
2 C. sugar
A few lemon or orange rinds
A cinnamon stick
Boil this mixture for ten minutes; allow to cool.

Brush tray with melted butter. Place 2 Fillo leaves on bottom of pan and brush or sprinkle with butter. Spread some chopped almonds or walnuts evenly over the Fillo. Place 2 more Filo leaves over top. Brush or sprinkle with melted butter and proceed as above until baking tray is filled. Place the last 3 sheets on top, baste with melted butter and with a pointed knife, score top sheets in square of diamond shapes. Bake in moderate oven (350 degrees) covered for ½ hour, uncover and then increase heat until top becomes golden brown. Bake for 1 hour, let cool and pour hot syrup over Baklava. Let it soak in. complete cuts on the scored lines and serve it cold.

CLAIRE BELFER'S TEATIME TASSIES

Shells: 1 3-oz. pkg. cream cheese, softened
           ½ butter, softened
           1 cup sifted flour

Mix the above ingredients together and chill for 1 hour.
Shape 2 doz. Inch balls, place in ungreased miniature muffin pans.
Press dough against bottom and sides,

Filling: ¾ cup brown sugar
           1 T. soft butter
           Dash salt
           1 t. vanilla
           1 egg
           2/3 cup chopped pecans divided in half

Beat together brown sugar, butter, salt, vanilla, egg until smooth. Then add 1/3
cup of pecans. Add filling to each cup. Top with remaining 1/3 cup pecans.
Bake 325 degrees for 25 minutes or until filling is set. Remove from pan when
cool.

ELAINE SELANDER'S UNCOOKED ORANGE COOKIES

1 # crushed vanilla wafers
1# powdered sugar
½ C. butter
½ C. crushed nuts
½ C. Angel Flake Coconut
1- 6 oz can frozen orange juice – do not dilute

Cream butter, add rest of ingredients and just enough orange juice to roll into
balls. Roll balls into powdered sugar, coconut and chopped nuts.

SUGAR COOKIES A LA SUE ROSE

I was born on Valentine's Day. The whole world celebrated! When I joined the staff at Forest Hills Northern High School, I met a beautiful, talented, with-it woman who taught art and had been single handedly responsible for augmenting the art department so that when she left, there were two and a half teachers. She was quite amazing. She could do anything including baking and decorating heart cookies for my birthday celebration. Here is her recipe

2/3 C. shortening
¾ C. sugar
1 t. vanilla or almond extract
1 egg
4 t. milk
2 C. sifted flour
1 ½ t. baking powder
¼ t. salt

Cream together shortening, sugar, vanilla and egg. Stir in milk. Add dry ingedients and mix well. Roll into ball and chill one hour. Roll out 1/8th inch thick and cut into shapes. Bake at 375 for 8 minutes.

BANANA OATMEAL COOKIES

Back in the late 1960s, I taught 38 students who were in both grades 3 and 4. I loved it. Too many kids in one room, many of whom had lots of problems—and back then I thought that I could fix every one of them! Well, I tried. . . it was what was then called the ghetto and race wars were raging in neighborhoods all over the country. I still loved it. The books were very old and outdated so I improvised, did lots of art projects, played classical music to calm them down and then went home to my own son, Hal, whom my students thought was named Hell. No comment! One of the boys named Michael McNamara who now must be in his mid-fifties wrote out this recipe for me and I have treasured it all these years. Enjoy:

1 ½ C. sifted flour
½ t. soda
1 t. salt
¼ t. nutmeg
¾ t. cinnamon
¾ C.shortening

1 C. sugar
1 egg
1 C. mashed bananas (2-3)
1 ¾ cup oatmeal
½ C. chopped nuts

Sift flour, soda, salt nutmeg, and cinnamon together. Beat shortening until creamy. Add sugar gradually and bet until light and fluffy. Add egg and beat again. Add mashed bananas, oatmeal and chopped nuts. Mix, then add dry ingredients. Drop by teaspoon onto ungreased sheet 1 ½ inches apart. Bake at 375 for about 15 minutes. Remove from pan at once.

CARAMEL COOKIES

I lived in Portland, Oregon for a year. When people asked why I was moving so far away from my home, I answered that it was as far from Grand Rapids, Michigan as I could get without falling into the ocean. I met some terrific people there. One of them named Inez took a 7 A.M. aerobics class at the Nautilus Plus gym where I worked from 5 A.M. to 9A.M . . Well, I'm a morning person and quite frankly I was not ready to retire from the working world. She gave me this wonderful cookie recipe; I have this to remember her by and am ever so grateful.

60 light caramels
1 pkg. German chocolate cake mix
¾ C. butter
¾ C. evaporated milk
1 C. semi-sweet chocolate chips
½ C. evaporated milk
1 C. chopped nuts

Combine caramels and ½ cup milk. Cook over low heat, stirring until melted. Set aside.

Grease and flour 9x13 pan. Combine cake mix, melted butter, 1/3 cup evaporated milk and nuts. Press ½ of the dough into the pan. Reserve rest for topping. Bake at 350 for 8 minutes. Sprinkle chocolate pieces over warm baked crust, then spread caramel mix over the chocolate pieces. Crumble the rest of the dough over the caramel layer and return to oven and bake 18-20 minutes longer.

Cool slightly, then refrigerate for 30 minutes to set carmel. Cut into bars.

MERINGUE NESTS

I am not sure why I am entering this recipe except that it came from a friend of my mother's and I was quite fond of her. Erna Kalkstine must have cooked and stirred and lived in Whitehall, Michigan where mom conned her out of this recipe for me to make.

2 egg whites
1/8 t. cream of tarter
Pinch of salt
½ C. sugar
½ t. vanilla
½ C. chopped nuts
Coconut

Beat eff whites and cream of tarter until stiff, but not dry. Fold in sugar, 1 T. at a time. Add vanilla and fastly the nuts or coconut. Drop by 1 t. full or form larger net with spoon on a brown paper li9ned cookie sheet. Bake at 275° for 40 minutes.

THUMBPRINT COOKIES

Makes about 4 ½ dozen. These classic cookies get their name from the method of using a thumb to create a round depression. The hole can be filled with any preserves you like.

¾ C. (1 and a half sticks) unsalted butter
½ C. sugar
2 eggs, lightly beaten
1 t. vanilla extract
½ t. ground cinnamon
¼ t. salt
2 C. all-purpose flour
2/3 C. preserves of your choice

Preheat oven to 400. In a large bowl with electric mixer, beat butter until creamy. qbout 30 seconds. Add sugar and beat until light and fluffy, 1 to 2 minutes. Gradually beat in eggs, vanilla extract, cinnamon and salt. Stir in flour until soft dough forms.

Spoon dough into a large pastry bag fitted with a plain ½ inch tip. Pipe 1 ½ inch rounds, 1 inch apart, on 2 large ungreased baking sheets. Press lightly floured thumb into center of each round, making a deep depression.

Bake cookies until golden, 7 to 10 minutes. Remove baking sheets to wire racks to cool slightly. Then, using a metal pancake turner, remove cookies to wire racks to cool completely.

In a small saucepan over low heat, heat preserves until just beginning to bubble. Using a small teaspoon, spoon a little preserve into each indentation while cookies are still warm. Allow cookies and jam to set and cook completely. Store in airtight containers in single layers.

RICH CARDAMOM COOKIES

These rich cookies are flavored with cardamom, a favorite Scandinavian spice.

2 C. cake flour
4 t. ground cardamom
¼ t. salt
¾ C. (1 and a half sticks) unsalted butter, softened
½ C. superfine sugar
½ C. sliced or flaked almonds

To decorate:

1/3 C. confectioners' sugar
1 ½ t. cardamom
Sliced or flaked almonds

Preheat oven to 375. Grease 2 large baking sheets. Into a medium bowl, sift together flour, cardamom and salt.

In a large bowl with electric mixer, beat butter until creamy. 30 seconds. Gradually add sugar and continue beating until light and fluffy, 1 to 2 minutes. On low speed, gradually beat in flour mixture until well blended; then stir in sliced or flaked almonds.

Into a small bowl, sift together confectioners' sugar and cardamom. Using a tablespoon, scoop out dough and roll into 1 ½ inch balls. Drop balls, one at a time into sugar-spice mixture, rolling to coat well.

Place 1 ½ inches apart on baking sheets. Dip bottoms of a glass into sugar mixture, and flatten cookies to ½ inch. Press 2 or 3 sliced or flaked almonds onto tops of cookies.

Bake cookies until golden brown, 12 to 14 minutes, rotating baking sheets from top to bottom shelf and from to back halfway through cooking time. Remove baking sheets to wire racks to cool, 2 to 3 minutes. Then, using a thing metal palette knife, remove cookies to wire racks to cool completely.

Store in airtight containers.

IMPERIAL COOKIES

As a high school counselor, I had the delight of meeting all kinds of kids from varied backgrounds. Many loved to share their recipes with me (quickly written on their notebook paper or backs of napkins) which of course have immortalized them in my book forever. I can see Nancy O'Betts' smile and feel her wonderful wit as I make her recipe for cookies every Christmas.

2 Sticks Imperial margarine (room temperature)
1 C. of sugar.
1 ½ C. flour
1 t. soda
1 t. vanilla or almond extract

Beat sugar and oil together for 15 minutes, adding sugar gradually. Add other ingredients to sugar and oil after beating for 15 minutes. Sprinkle with holiday colored sugars.

Bake at 300 degrees for 15- 20 minutes.

ORIGINAL TOLL HOUSE COOKIES

Before the dairy case carried chocolate chip cookies, there were these— and the recipe is divine.

2 ½ C. UNSIFTED flour
1 t. baking soda
1 t. salt
1 C. butter, softened
¾ C. sugar
1 C. chopped nuts

¾ C. firmly packed brown sugar
1 t. vanilla
2 Eggs
1 12 oz. Nestle Semi Sweet Real Chocolate
      Morsel pkg. (2 cups)

Preheat oven to 375 degrees. In small bowl, combine flour, baking soda and salt, set aside. In large bowl combine butter, sugar, brown sugar and vanilla; beat until creamy. Beat in eggs. Gradually add flour mixture, mix well. Stir in Nestle Semi Sweet Real Chocolate Morsels and nuts. Drop by teaspoonful onto ungreased cookie sheet. Bake at 375 degrees 8 – 10 minutes. Makes 100 2-inch cookies.

SUGAR COOKIES

When Ed Boardwell, Cousin Margo's husband, went deer hunting in November, I would point my car north and stay with her for a long weekend. We had all sorts of projects to do. One of them was to bake Christmas cookies. She would roll these out, cut the pattern and bake them while I would do the decorating.

1 c. butter (2 sticks, use the real stuff)
2 c. granulated sugar
¾ t. baking soda
½ t. salt

1 t. vanilla
3 eggs, beaten
3 ½ C. all purpose flour
2 t. baking powder

Cream butter and sugar. Blend in baking soda, salt and vanilla. Add eggs and beat until smooth. Combine flour and baking powder and add to creamed mixture, mixing until very smooth. Chill dough until firm enough to roll out on floured pastry surface. Preheat oven to 450 degrees. Cut into shapes with cookie cutters. Place on greased baking sheets. Bake 8 minutes until cookies are golden.

AUSTRIAN CRESCENTS

This is a typical Viennese cookie. The addition of ground almonds makes the dough very short and they melt in your mouth.

Preheat oven to 325°. Grease 2 large baking sheets.

½ C. (1 stick) unsalted butter, softened
1 C. all-purpose flour
½ C. slivered blanched almonds, finely ground
¼ t. almond extract
Confectioners' sugar for dusting

In a large bowl, with electric mixer, beat butter until creamy, 30 seconds. On low speed, gradually beat in flour, ground almonds, salt and almond extract, until a soft dough forms.

Using a teaspoon, scoop out dough and, using your lightly floured fingers, shape into 1 ½ - inch crescents. Place crescents 1 inch apart on baking sheets. Bake until crescents are firm and just lightly golden (cookies should be pale), about 18 to 20 minutes, rotating from top to bottom shelf and from front to back halfway through cooking time.

Remove baking sheets to wire racks to cool slightly. Then, using a metal pancake turner or palette knife, remove cookies to wire racks to cool completely. Arrange crescents on wire rack, and dust lightly with confectioners' sugar. Store in airtight containers. If you like, redust with confectioners' sugar before serving.

MRS. FIELD'S FAMOUS CHOCOLATE CHIP COOKIES – 112 cookies

Don't ask me how or where my daughter-in-law got a hold of this recipe, but here it is.

Cream: 2 C. butter
                    2 C. sugar
                    2 C. brown sugar (packed)

Add: 4 eggs
        2 t. vanilla

In a separate bowl, place 4 C. flour
                          5 C. oatmeal
Put this mixture into blender in small amounts. Blend until it turns to powder.
                1 t. salt
                2 t. baking powder (add a pinch more for softness
                2 t. baking soda
Mix all ingredients then add:
                24 oz. chocolate chips
                1 – 8 oz. Hershey's chocolate bar, grated
                2 to 3 C. chopped nuts

Shape into balls and place on ungreased cookie sheet. Preheat oven to 375 degrees so that it is very hot before putting cookies in. Bake about 6 minutes (half batch cookies are softer).

BUTTER DREAMS COOKIES

Mix well together:

        1 C. butter
        1 t. vanilla
        ½ C. sifted powdered sugar

Mix together: 2 ¼ C. sifted flour
                ¼ t. salt

Stir in: ¾ C. finely chopped nuts and mix well

Chill dough. Roll in 1" balls. Place 2 ½ " apart on greased baking sheet. Bake at 375 for 8-10 or until set and light brown. White still warm, roll in powdered sugar. Cool. Roll in sugar again. Makes about 4 dozen cookies.

LEMON BARS

2 C. flour
½ C. confectioners sugar
1 C. butter

Filling:
4 eggs, beaten
2 C. sugar
Dash salt
6 T. fresh lemon juice
¼ C. flour
1 t. baking powder
Confectioners sugar

Preheat oven to 350. Grease 9 x 13 inch pan. Combine flour and confectioners sugar; cut in butter. Pat into pan. Bake 20 minutes. For filling: Combine eggs, sugar, salt, lemon juice, flour and baking powder. Pour over hot crust; bake 25 min.. Cool. Sprinkle with confectioners sugar.

HEATH BAR DESSERT

2 half pints whipping cream
6 Heath Bars chilled
2 pkg. lady fingers

Whip cream sweetened with 1 t. vanilla and sugar (in today's world, throw the vanilla into some Dream Whip). Line bottom of 9x13 pan with split lady fingers. Fold crushed Heath Bars into whipped cream. Put half of mixture on top of lady fingers. Put another layer of lady fingers on top. Top with rest of whipped cream- heath mixture. Chill. Serves 10-12.

DIRT PUDDING

I had this once at a luncheon and it was a hit when the hostess served this dessert in plastic flower pots into which small toy shovels had been placed. (If I remember, she also added an artificial flower which stood straight up and caused a lot of comments) Remember to cover the hole in bottom of pot with aluminum

1 Regular sized pkg. Oreo cookies
8 oz. cream cheese, softened
1 lg. pkg. instant vanilla pudding
1-1/2 C. milk
1 C. powdered sugar
1 small container Cool Whip

1) Crush cookies with rolling pin or blender
2) In mixer blend cream cheese, pudding mix, milk, and powdered sugar
3) Fold in Cool Whip
4) Alternate layers of pudding mix and cookie crumbs – end with crumbs

.

PEGGY HISS'S APPLE DUMPLINGS

Peggy is the mother of my daughter-in law, Debra. She is a master cook and this is one of her recipes I had to beg Debra for. They are to die for!

Bake at 375 degrees for 35 – 35 minutes

Pie Crust

1 C. lard
1 T. vinegar
¾ t. salt
½ C. water (use warm water if lard is hard (most store bought lard is hard)
3 C. flour

Mix lard, water, salt and vinegar together thoroughly (mix with mixer or whisk – and see note above with ingrediants). Roll out a ball (a little larger than a baseball) and cut into fourths.   Add flour and mix by hand.

Apple Dumplings and Sauce

¼ t. nutmeg
Red food coloring
McIntosh Apples
4 T. butter

2 C. sugar
2 C, water
¼ t. cinnamon

Combine sugar, water, cinnamon, nutmeg, food coloring. Bring to a boil. Add butter. Roll our each fourth of pie crust and mound with apples, Sprinkle with sugar, cinnamon and a dash of nutmeg. Dot with butter. Fold up 4 corners and push dough corners together. Move dumplings w/ a spatula onto an ungreased pan about 7-8 dumplings per pan. Spoon sauce over dumplings, completely moisturizing each dumpling. Sprinkle lightly w/sugar.

May use other sorts of apples about 2 to 2 ½ lbs. per single batch.

ENGLISH TRIFLE

This dish dates back to the 18th century and was served to the most critical guest who raved about its goodness. We are still raving. I had a wonderful secretary named Carole Wheeler. She was English by heritage and was going to celebrate a birthday in December so I was determined to make her a trifle. I fell, however, coming into the school building in November and tore a ligament in my right hand which was put into a cast at Blodgett Hospital. Needless to say, a cook is never discouraged so I asked my mother to do a lot of the stirring and it was she who helped me put this delicious surprise for Carole together. It looks beautiful and is ever so easy. Try it!

1 store bought sponge cake
1 C. raspberry preserves
1 C. Dry Sherry
1 pkg. family-size vanilla pudding (following directions for the making of)
Large container of Cool-whip
Strawberries
Sliced, toasted almonds

Buy one sponge cake and cut it in thirds (layers), top to bottom; this can be dried out for several hours. Spread bottom 1/3 cake with ½ cup of raspberry preserves and continue to 2nd layer with another ½ cup of preserves.

After placing the top layer on the 2nd layer, press down (GENTLY) to bind it) Cut the layers into large cubes and put them into large mixing bowl. Sprinkle with dry sherry and toss the cubes to distribute the sherry evenly. Spoon ½ of the sherry-soaked cubes into a deep glass bowl. After following directions on a family- size vanilla pudding box for that ingredient, throw that in on top. Sprinkle with remainder of cubes and top with a large container of Cool-Whip. Top that with 8 to 10 washed and hulled strawberries and 1 cup of sliced, toasted almonds.

BITE SIZE CHEESE CAKE

This recipe was given to me by my neighbor, Dr. Marcia Fetters who teaches in the education department of Western Michigan University and who has an interesting background in the Amish faith. .

A delicious bite size version of a classic dessert that can be made with aa variation of toppings to suit anyone! Easy to make, short bake time, and a great little dessert or snack for those who monitor their portion sizes.   Ahhhhh, that would be me!

Crust: 1 cup graham cracker crumbs
                1/8 C. sugar
                ¼ C. butter, melted

Filling: 16 oz cream cheese
                1 t. vanilla
                2 eggs
                ½ C. sugar
                1 can pie filling, any flavor

Preparation:
1) Preheat oven to 340 degrees
2) Line mini muffin pan with mini muffin cups.
3) Combine graham cracker crumbs, sugar, and melted butter.
4) Add 2 t. crumb mix to each cup. It's ok to be generous.
5) Firmly press down in cup to pack the crumbs.
6) Combine cream cheese, vanilla, eggs and sugar. Mix well
7) Add 1 T. of cream cheese mixture to each cup.
8) Bake 14 minutes.
9) Top with a dollop of pie filling flavor of your choice.
10) Cool at least one hour prior to serving.

For Topping: Combine sour cream, sugar and vanilla in small bowl. Spread over surface of warm cheesecake. Return to 350 degree oven and bake for 5 minutes. Cool on wire rack. Remove sides of pan and chill several hours or overnight in refrigerator. Spread the any remaining whipped cream decoratively around edge of pie. The end result is worth the effort.

TIRAMISU

3 C. mascarpone
1 ½ C. confectioners' sugar
¼ C. Marsala
¾ C. double cream
2/3 C. water
5 t. instant espresso
1 store-bought butter pound cake

In a medium bowl, use electric mixer set on medium speed to beat the mascarpone cheese, c cup confectioners' sugar and marsala until well blended. Add cream and beat until fluffy, about 1 minute. Set aside.

In a small saucepan over high heat combine water, remaining ½ cup of confectioners' sugar and espresso powder. Bring to a boil. Stir occasionally. Remove from heat and cool. Slice pound cake ¼ inch thick. Have a 2 quart oval or rectangular glass or ceramic dish. Arrange slices of cake in a single layer over bottom of dish. Trimming to fit. Brush half of the cooled espresso mixture over cake. Spread half of the mascarpone mixture even over the top. Then repeat and do the second lay. Brush espresso over cake slices and top with remaining cheese. Cover with plastic and refrigerate until firm. Before serving sift cocoa even on top. Use a large scoop to serve on plates.

SWEDISH ROSETTES (CRULLERS)

Aunty Greet, Margo's mother, married a Swede so she gleaned a lot of recipes which had come from the old country. She made them by the score as does her daughter today. Margo used to make a big basket of these Swedish treats for my brother, Mack, at the holiday time which put him in seventh heaven.

Makes 40

1 C. flour
2 eggs (mix very little and stir slowly)
1 C. milk
1/3 cup sugar
1 t. of salt

2 T. salad oil
1 t. vanilla, lemon or almond extract

You will need a rosette iron which can be found at a specialty shop, hardware store, general store etc. as well as an oil thermometer.

In a deep bowl, mix eggs, milk and flavoringl. Sift together flour, salt, and sugar; add a little at a time into egg mixture. Mix thoroughly and pour into a shallow bowl. Let mixture sit to eliminate bubbles.

Place fat (Crisco) in a deep fryer or sauce pan. Place rosette iron in fat. Heat slowly until fat reaches 360 degrees. If you don't have a thermometer, test heat with a piece of white bread – it should be golden within a few seconds after dropping in fat.

When fat is proper temperature, remove iron, drain quickly on absorbent paper, dip into battle (well stirred) so the batter coats bottom and sides of iron, keeping top free of batter. Dip quickly into hot fat a few seconds. Batter will drop off ironl. Turn with slotted spoon and remove. Place on paper towels, sprinkle right away with powdered sugar. Be sure to put the iron back in fat after cruller falls off.

Store in an open basket with a tea towel loosely covering it. If you put the ro-settes in an air tight container, they will shrink and be an awful mess.

CHOCOLATE CARAMEL SURPRISE BROWNIES

1 German chocolate cake mix
1/3 C. pet milk
¾ C. butter, melted
Mix the above by hand. Pour ½ into greased 9x13 pan. Bake 10 minutes at 325.

14 Oz. pkg. caramels
1 C. chocolate chips
1 C. salted peanuts

Melt caramels w/ 1/3 cup more of pet milk. Pour over baked mixture and sprinkle w/ chocolate chips and peanuts. Spread rest of batter over top. Bake 18-20 minutes.

You may want to chop the nuts a bit. These are like snickers. Good!!!!

COUSIN MARGO'S NO SUGAR PEANUT BUTTER COOKIES

1 C. peanut butter, sugarless
1 C. Splenda
1 Egg
1 t. vanilla

Mix and roll into balls, criss-cross with a fork.
Bake 18 minutes @ 350 °
Let rest on cookie sheet for 5 minutes.

ELAINE HOFFMAN'S POPPY SEED COOKIES

Elaine had been raised Orthodox Jewish on Long Island in New York. I met her as a learned colleague who taught history, government and ethics. She had a magnificent passion for life and immediately became a good friend and actually ended up marrying a friend of mine. They moved to San Diego and I never heard from either of them again. I do, however, share her recipe for poppy seed cookies right out of her Jewish cookbook . So enjoy!

3 Eggs
½ C. oil
½ C. sugar
3 C. flour
Pinch of salt
1/3 C. poppy seeds, washed and soaked in warm water,
2 t. baking powder
1 t. vanilla or almond extract

Beat eggs and sugar, add oil, poppy seeds and flavoring. Mix in flour thoroughly. Roll into a log and chill. Cut into 1/8 inch thickness and place on a greased cookie sheet, sprinkle with sugar. Pop into a 375 degree oven until brown, about 10 minutes.

UNBAKED COOKIES

2 C. sugar
½ C. milk
½ C. cocoa
½ C. butter
½ T. vanilla

Boil the above ingredients for 2 minutes

Add:
3 C. oats
½ C. crunchy peanut butter
¼ C. nuts

Roll into balls and eat, eat, eat!

SUE DUFF'S MOTHER'S GINGER SNAPS

This is another recipe that is over 100 years old. . . .And spectacular!

¾ C. Crisco, butter flavored
1 C. granulated sugar
1 egg
¼ C. molasses
2 C. sifted flour
¼ t. salt
2 t. baking soda
¾ t. cinnamon
1/8 t. Allspice
2 t. ginger

Chill dough about 10 minutes. Roll in little balls, dip in sugar (granulated) and place on cookie sheet. Leave room between cookies, then flatten the cookies with the bottom of a glass dipped in sugar. Bake at 350 degrees for about 8 minutes.   Serves many.

SWEDISH GINGER SNAPS - From Elaine Selander

Cream together: 2/3 C. shortening
                     ¾ C. sifted light brown sugar, firmly packed
                     2 T. molasses
3 T. boiled, cooled water
1 t. grated lemon rind
2 ¼ C. sifted all-purpose flour
1 t. baking soda
1 T. cinnamon
1 ½ t. cloves
1 t. pulverized or ground cardamom seeds

Incorporate all. Chill. Roll out thinly and use a cookie cutter to design cookie. Bake 350 degrees for 8 to 10 minutes.

MOM ROSSITER'S STARLIGHT SURPRISE MINT COOKIES

Marianna Rossiter was my "very best friend" when we were going up. We were inseparable. Her mother was a fabulous cook and Marianna would boast that she was the best cook in town. Well, Cousin Margo would tell her differently, but whatever! Mrs. Rossiter would make this cookie recipe on my birthday and I knew that it was the best thing that I would get. Did I share them? I should say not. I hid them! When I was about to be married, she threw me a shower, gave me cookie tins and the treasured recipe for these cookies. I still have the 70 year old recipe written in her hand. I share here.

Sift together :   3 C. flour
                      1 t. soda
                      ½ t. salt

Cream 1 cup butter (half shortening may be used).
Add gradually 1 C. sugar
                ½ C. brown sugar
Cream well

Add: 2 eggs unbeaten
      2 T. water
      1 t. vanilla
Beat well
Add dry ingredients. Mix thoroughly, cover and refrigerate at least 2 hours.

1 pkg. (9 oz.) solid chocolate mint candy wafers (I cannot locate these any-where so I buy chocolate candy wafers at the Candy Lady's store and douse a cotton ball in mint extract, throw them all in a plastic bag for a few days so that the flavor is imparted to the chocolate).

Enclose each wafer in about 1 T. of dough. Place on a greased baking sheet about 2 inches apart. Top each with a walnut half. Bake 375 degrees for 10 to 12 minutes.

EASY LEMON SQUARES

I had a wonderful neighbor in my early years of homemaking by the name of Claire Belfer. She and her husband, Harvey, would have my sons and me over for Hanukah each year when they lived across the street from us. I associate a lot of things she cooked as Claire's Jewish food. She was a superlative cook and we still connect once a year, she from West Palm Beach and me from Kalamazoo and rattle on about philosophy.

Base:
1 Pkg. lemon pudding including yellow cake mix
2 C. crushed corn flakes cereal
1/2 C. firmly packed brown sugar
1/3 C. chopped nuts
½ C. butter, softened

Filling:
3 Oz. package lemon pudding/pie filling (not instant)
14 Oz. can sweetened condensed milk (not evaporated)
¾ t. lemon extract

Glaze:
1 C. powdered sugar, sifted
¼ t. lemon extract
3-5 t. water

Heat oven to 350 degrees. Generously grease 15 x 10 x 1 inch baking pan. In a large bowl, combine base ingredients at low speed till crumbly. Reserve 1 ½ c mixture for topping. Press remaining mixture in bottom of greased pan. In small bowl, combine all filling mixture - - pour over base evenly, gently spreading. Spread with reserved crumb mixture. Bake 350 degrees 20 – 30 minutes until golden brown. Loosen edges. In small bowl, blend the glaze and drizzle over warm bars. Cool completely. Cut into bars. Makes 48.

22's SURPRIZE

1 C. cooked white or brown rice (micro extra to make rice soft)
1 Box vanilla pudding mix (the kind to cook on stove)
2 C. milk
1 C. ice cream
¼ C. chopped pecans
¼ t. cinnamon
1/8 t. nutmeg

In a saucepan, put in rice, pudding mix, milk, ice cream and cinnamon. Heat on stove, stirring until it boils. Remove from stove and put in service dishes or larger dish until ready to serve. Before serving, sprinkle some nutmeg on the top.

NOODLE KUGEL

I wasn't sure whether to put this in main meals or desserts and so here it is in desserts. Florence Obstfeld, my best Oregon buddy, finally admitted after a year of us going down town to Symphony Hall and eating across the street in a Jewish deli (my idea, not hers) that she really didn't like Jewish food – how do I keep my friends? Furthermore, my eldest son, Hal, requested this recipe.

16 oz. broad egg noodles
4 T. butter, melted
1 Lb. cottage cheese
1 Lb. sour cream
4 Eggs beaten
½ C. sugar
1 T. vanilla extract
1 C. crushed cornflakes
1 t. cinnamon
¼ - ½ C. sugar
Some people add a small can of pineapple and some chopped up nuts

(continued on next page)

1) Cook noodles, drain and rinse w/ cold water.
2) In a large bowl mix the noodles w/the melted butter, cheeses, eggs, sugar and vanilla
3) Pour into a greased 9x13" pan
4) In a separate bowl. Mix the cornflakes, cinnamon, and sugar – sprinkle this on top of Noodles mixture.
5) Bake for about 1 hour @ 350 degrees or until top is brown.

BANANA'S FOSTER

A staple at Brennan's in New Orleans in the French Quarter since 1951 and so fun to watch the staff make. Try this on your family or guests.

4 Servings

¼ C. (1/2 stick) butter
1 C. brown sugar
½ C. cinnamon
¼ C. banana liqueur
4 Bananas cut lengthwise, then halved
¼ C. dark rum
4 Scoops vanilla ice cream

Combine the butter, sugar and cinnamon in a flambé pan or skillet. Place the pan on low heat on an alcohol burner or top of the stove and cook until sugar dissolves. Stir in banana liqueur, then place bananas in pan. When bananas sections begin to soften, add the rum. Continue to cook until the rum is hot, stand back and ignite. When flames subside, lift the banana pieces out and place 4 pieces over each portion of ice cream. Generously spoon sauce over each serving and serve immediately. Oh Yum!

APPLE DAPPLE

My Aunt Betty (Cousin, Nick Nichols' mother) who was the Margrave family's 'little thing', weighing in at about 90 pounds, had a great sense of clothes taste, and fashion finesse, It was she who gave a shower for me when I was about to be married. This is the great dessert she served.

¾ C. sugar
2 Eggs, beaten
½ C. sifted flour
1 ½ t. Baking powder
½ t. salt
½ C. chopped nuts
1 C. diced tart apples (Granny Smith would be great)
1 t. vanilla or ½ t. almond
Whipped cream or ice cream

Add sugar to eggs. Beat well. Sift dry ingredients and blend into egg mixture. Fold in nuts, apples and flavoring. Pour into buttered pie tin. Bake at 350 degrees for 35-40 minutes. Cool. Cut into wedges. Cover with whip cream or Ice cream. Serves 6.

MOUNDS CANDY

¾ C. hot mashed potatoes
4 C. flaked coconut
4 C. confectioners sugar
¼ to ½ t. almond extract
1-12 Oz. pkg. chocolate chips

Mix well and chill overnight. Shape into small balls, about marble size and chill several more hours. Doing only a few at a time, leaving the rest in refrigeration, dip with fork, toothpick, or turkey dressing nail into 12 ounces of melted chocolate chips and 1/16 to 1/8 bar of melted paraffin (gives chocolate shine). Keep the mixture of chocolate and paraffin over boiling water while dipping. Place on wax paper until cool. You may need more chocolate chips. It depends on how well you let the candy drip before you put it on the wax paper

ENGLISH TOFFEE

Buttered 9x13 pan

Combine in saucepan, stir until butter melts, then cook and stir to 320 degrees on candy thermometer:

> 1 C. sugar
> 1 C. butter
> 3 T. water

Add 1 t. vanilla and QUICKLY pour in thin layer into buttered pan and lay broken chocolate bars (8) over hot candy.
Spread evenly over then sprinkle with ¾ cup chopped pecans.
When cool, break into pieces.

CHOCOLATE PIZZA

Quietly given to me by Connie Kubicki, a colleague from St. Joseph, Michigan, one wonderful Christmas. I begged for the recipe on hands and knees so she gave it to me.

2 pkgs. (6 squares each) Bakers premium white chocolate
1 pkg. (12 oz.) Bakers's Semi-Sweet Real Chocolate Chips
1 C. peanuts
2 C. mini marshmallows
1 C. Rice Krispies
½ C. coconut
red & green candied cherries

Melt chips and white chocolate in large saucepan on low heat. Stir in marshmallows, cereal, and peanuts. Pour onto greased 12-inch pizza pan. Decorate with the coconut, red and green cherries melted white chocolate or almond bark. Store at room temperature. Makes 10 – 12 servings.

Gift giving: For smaller pizzas, spoon chocolate mixture onto greased cookie sheet, forming 3 (7-inch) or 4 (6-inch) circles with back of wooden spoon. Continue as directed. Place on cardboard circle ;wrap in colorful cellophane and tie with a bow OR get some pizza boxes, place chocolate pizza inside and tie with a beautiful bow.

Notes

This 'n That

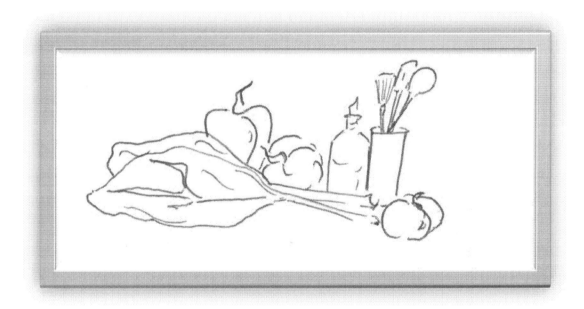

TASTEFUL KITCHEN KLASSICS

Flavored Butters and Spreads

For a delightful experience, try these flavorful butters and spreads atop bagels, French toast, muffins, pancakes or waffles. Place in a mason jar, tie with home-spun fabric and attach the recipe to make a tasteful gift.

Honey Walnut Spread

8 oz. package of cream cheese, softened
½ C. honey
¼ C. coarsely chopped walnuts

In a medium bowl, combine cream cheese and honey, mix well. Stir in walnuts, cover and refrigerate. Yield: 1 cup

Cranberry Orange Spread

8 oz. package cream cheese, softened
¼ C. whole cranberry sauce
1 t. orange juice
½ t. fresh grated orange peel

In a small food processor bowl, combine all ingredients. Process until well blended. Yield: 1 cup

Pumpkin Butter

2 C. mashed, cooked pumpkin (may use canned)   1 ½ C. sugar
½ t. ground cinnamon   1/8 t. ground nutmeg
1/8 t. lemon juice   1/8 t. ground cloves

In a medium saucepan, combine all ingredients; stir. Bring to a boil, reduce heat and simmer uncovered for 30 minutes or until thickened, stirring frequently. Cover and refrigerate. Yield: 2 cups

Food Processor Peanut Butter

2 C. roasted shelled peanuts
1 T. Peanut oil
½ t. salt (omit if salted peanuts are used)

Using the metal blade, process ingredients continuously for 2 to 3 minutes. The ground peanuts will form a ball which will slowly disappear. Continue to process until the desired consistency is obtained. If necessary, stop machine and scrape sides of container with rubber spatula.

For crunchy peanut butter, stir in ½ C. chopped roasted peanuts after the process is completed.

Yields 1 C. creamy or 1 ½ cups crunchy peanut butter

Store in a tightly closed container in the refrigerator. Oil may rise to the top. If this occurs, stir before using. You can do the same with almonds.

SEASONED SALT

¾ C. kosher salt
2 ¼ t. dry mustard
1 ½ t. celery seed, ground
4 ½ t. onion powder
¼ t. chili powder
¾ t. paprika
¼ t. cayenne pepper
¼ t. turmeric, ground

Combine all of the ingredients in a processor and mix on medium speed until mixture is of desired fineness. Spoon into jar with tight fitting lid. Store in cool place as you would any salt. Use in place of regular salt to season meats, seafood, vegetables, salad dressings etc.
Makes about 1 cup seasoned salt.

HOMEMADE BISCUIT MIX

3 ¾ C. shortening (butter flavored is best) 5 Lbs. self-rising flour. Cut shortening into flour. Store in closed canister. Use for biscuits, coffee cakes, quick bread, pancakes, .muffins, or any recipe calling for commercial biscuit mix. (Yields 6 pounds mix)

TURKEY DATA WHICH SHOULD BE NOTED

Buying: What size will I need? If you are buying a ready to cook, under 12 lbs, allow ¾ - 1 pound per serving, over 12 lbs. ½ - ¾ pounds per serving. Turkeys over 12 pounds generally have more meat, less bone.

Ready-to-Cook Turkey	Number of Servings
8 - 12 Lbs.	10 – 20
12 – 16 Lbs.	20 – 32
16 – 20 Lbs.	32 – 40

How do I thaw a frozen turkey? Leave bird in its original body wrap. Place on tray in refrigerator. Allow 1 to 3 days for thawing process. (24 hours per 6 pounds).

How much stuffing do I need? Allow 1 cup per pound of turkey.

When should I stuff the bird? Not until it is time to put it in the oven. Early stuffing can contaminate and cause those eating it to be very ill.

How long should I roast the turkey and at what temperature? Set oven at 325 degrees, place, breast side up, on rack in shallow roasting pan lined with foil. When bird is 2/3 done, cover with tent of heavy-foil. Roast until thermometer reads 185 degrees. If you do not have a thermometer, check the thickest part of the drumstick; it should feel very soft when pressed. Remove from oven and let stand 20 minutes, covered, for easier carving and a juicier bird.

How do I time roasting?

Ready-to-cook weight	Cooking time guide
8 to 12 Lbs.	2 ½ to 3 hours
12 to 16 Lbs.	3 to 3 ¾ hours
16 to 20 Lbs.	3 ¾ to 4 ½ hours

OTHER NOTES OF INTEREST AND HELP

Substitutions

1 t. allspice . ... ½ t. cinnamon plus
1/8 t. cloves plus
¼ t. nutmeg

1 t. baking powder. . . . . ¼ t. soda plus
½ t. cream of tartar

1 C. butter. . . . . 1 C. sweet milk plus
1 T. lemon juice or vinegar

1 square chocolate
(unsweetened). . . . . 3 T. cocoa plus
1 T. butter

1 6 oz. pkg. chocolate
(semi-sweet). . . . . 2 squares unsweetened chocolate plus
2 T. shortening plus
½ C. sugar

3 T. cocoa. . . . . 1 square unsweetened chocolate (omittng
1 Tb. butter)

¼ C. syrup +1 C.Splenda . . . . brown sugar

2/3 C. Splenda + 2 T. Corn starch . .powdered sugar

1 T. cornstarch . . . . .2 T. flour (for thickening) or 4 tsp. tapioca

¾ C. cracker crumbs. . . . . 1 C. bread crumbs

1 Whole egg. . . . . 2 yolks plus 1 T. water

1 C. flour, sifted. . . . . .1 C. plus 2 T. sifted cake flour

1 C. cake flour, sifted . . . . .1 C. minus 2 T. flour

1 C. self-rising flour. . . . . 1 C. flour and 1 ½ t. baking powder

1 Medium clove garlic . . . . ½ t. garlic powder plus 1/8 t. instant
flakes plus ½ t. salt (omitting other salt in
recipe)

1 T. fresh herb. . . . . 1 t. dried herbs

---

1 C. honey	3/4 C. sugar plus ¼ C. liquid
1 Medium lemon	2 to 3 T. juice or 1 ½ t. lemon flavoring
1 C. fresh milk	1/2 C. evaporated milk plus ½ C. water or 4 T. powdered milk dissolved in 1 C. water.
1 C. molasses	1 C. honey
1 t. dry mustard	1 T. prepared mustard
1 medium onion	2 T. instant, chopped or minced onion flakes or 1 ½ t. onion powder
1 t. poultry seasoning	¼ t. thyme plus ¾ t. sage seasoning
Pumpkin pie. Spices . . . . Spices	½ t. cinnamon plus ½ t. ginger ½ t. allspice plus 1/8 t. nutmeg
1 C. sour cream	1 C. evaporated milk or 1 C. heavy cream, plus 1 T. vinegar or 7/8 cup buttermilk & 3 T. butter
1 C. granulated sugar	1 C. light brown sugar, well packed
1 C. tomato catsup	1 C. tomato sauce plus 1/2 C. sugar plus 2 T. vinegar
1 C. tomato juice	1/2 C. tomato sauce plus ½ C. water
1 C. whipping cream	3/4 C. whole milk plus1/3 C. butter (only works if cream is going into recipe to be cooked or baked. Will not whip)

NOTE: These are extremely helpful substitutes if you are out of something and do not want to run to the store in the middle of cooking and stirring.

FLAVORED VINEGARS: A PUNGENT ELIXIR FROM AGES PAST

Making flavored vinegar:

White vinegar is better with delicate flavorings, through at times it may be a little acidic. Cider vinegar is good with many flavors, especially. Let your taste buds guide you.

The fastest way to make flavored vinegar is to heat the vinegar in a stainless steel or enamel pot until it is hot, but not to boiling. Pour the hot vinegar over the fruit, herbs, or spices. Cover with cheesecloth and let stand in a warm, dark place for one to two weeks. Then filter vinegar through paper coffee filters or several layers of cheesecloth and pour into clean bottles.

To make herb vinegar, start with about one cup lightly packed herbs leaves per quart of vinegar. If the leaves are chopped or crushed, they will release more of their essence than the whole leaves. Flower vinegars will take about the same ratio, through some of the more delicately scented ones may take as much as three or four cups of flower petals per quart of vinegar. Heat vinegar only to lukewarm for herb or flower vinegars. In making seed vinegars such as caraway or mustard, start with two to three tablespoons of seeds per quart of vinegar. Mash or crush them with a spoon or mortar and pestle. Spice vinegars usually take about the same ratio as seed vinegars, though the spices can usually be left whole. In both kinds, heating is needed to flavor the vinegar adequately.

To make fruit vinegars, about 1 pound of chopped or mashed fresh fruit, such as peaches, cherries, or apricots, will flavor a quart of vinegar nicely. If using berries, allow about a pint of blueberries or raspberries per quart. After you get the hang of this you will want to try your hand at mixing them, but that's for later.

LEMON GARLIC VINEGAR

Heat 1 Qt. white wine or distilled vinegar (do not boil); pour over peel of 2 lemons and 2 cloves garlic; crushed in a crock or jar. Let stand, covered, in a warm dark place 1 to 2 weeks. Check for flavor. Strain into clean bottles. Makes 1 quart.

GINGER VINEGAR

In food processor, process 4 to 6 Oz. fresh gingerroot. Heat 1 Qt. vinegar (do not boil). Pour over gingerroot in crock or jar. Cover tightly. Let stand in a warm, dark place for 1 to 2 weeks. Check flavor. Strain into clean bottles. Makes 1 quart.

TLC: A good squeeze of fresh lemon or a dash of wine will help any bottled dressing, mayonnaise, or leftover homemade dressing.

NASTURTIUM VINEGAR

Warm 1 qt. white vinegar to lukewarm. Place 1 C. nasturtium petals, 1 shallot, chopped, and 1 t. cracked peppercorns in jar, crush gently with wooden spoon. Add vinegar; cover tightly (if lid is metal, line with plastic wrap). Let stand in a warm place about 4 weeks. Strain into clean bottles, cork tightly. Makes 1 qt.

SPICY MARINATED VEGGIES

This is a recipe of daughter-in-law, Debra's mother, Peggy Hiss.

1 C. vinegar
1 C. water
2 t. salt
1 pouch crab and shrimp boil
6 pkts. Equal

Put vinegar, water and salt in pan and stir – put pouch in and bring to a boil- simmer for 5 full minutes. Remove pouch and squeeze all juice out of it. Dis- card pouch. Put in the 6 pkts. Equal and stir. Pour hot liquid over veggies. Cover and marinate 4 hours.

Green peppers	Red peppers	
Yellow peppers	Mushrooms	
Red and green onions	Carrots	
Broccoli	Cauliflower	Cherry tomatoes

BARBEQUE RELISH

This comes from daughter-in-law, Debra Hiss Brey's Grandmother Hiss

10 pints:
2x = single batch
1 Peck green tomatoes
6 Large onions
6 Red peppers
6 Green peppers

3x = single batch
4 ½ C. white sugar
1 Pt. vinegar
1 T. celery seed
1 t. ground cloves
1 t. ground cinnamon
1 t. tumeric

Mix above ingredients with drained vegetables, bring all to a boil; put in jars and seal. These should be run up to 5 lbs. in a pressure cooker and turned off.

AMISH BREAD AND BUTTER PICKLES

Another recipe from Helen Hiss, Debra Hiss Brey's Grandmother. Deb was raised in northern Indiana where the Amish flourish, though she was not Amish (Oh, and that's pronounced Ahh – mish). I love to go to Shipshewana, a short ride from Kalamazoo and observe Amish culture, full of recipes, fabulous cheeses and meats, quilts and beautiful handmade furniture. I am sure that living in Oregon where she lives with my son, Hal, she must have some fond memories of that culture.

30 Medium size cucumbers (1 gallon, sliced)
2 Large green or red peppers
½ C. salt
5 ½ C. + 2 Tbls. sugar
5 C. vinegar, apple cider 5% acidity

(continued on next page)

2 T. mustard seed
1 t. turmeric
1 Scant T. whole cloves

Slice cucumbers in rings – do not pare. Slice onions in rings. Cut peppers in fine strips. Dissolve salt in ice water and pour over sliced vegetables. Let stand 3 hours. Drain well.

Combine vinegar, sugar and spices and bring to a boil. Add drained vegetables and heat to boiling point – do not boil. Place in sterilized jars and seal.

PLUM GLAZE

Slowly heat: 1 C. plum jam until it melts

Stir in: 1 T. catsup
                          1 T. lemon or lime juice
                          2 t. lemon or lime peel
                          2 t. vinegar
                          1 t. grated fresh ginger or about ½ t. ground ginger
                          1/8 t. liquid hot pepper seasoning
                          ¼ t. dry mustard
                          ¼ t. ground cinnamon
                          1/8 t. ground cloves

Use for duck or in Asian cooking.

ORANGE SAUCE
May also use as a fondue dip.

4 Large oranges (use the juice)
2 Medium sized lemons (use the juice)
4 t. arrowroot   1 T butter
2/3 C. water   1/3 C. sugar

Mix together in a small pan and heat to boiling, stirring. Grate peel from 2 oranges and 1 lemon and incorporate at the end.

SEASONED BUTTERS

WHIPPED, CHILLED BUTTERS

GARLIC BUTTER: Combine ½ C. (1/4 lb) butter at room temperature, 2 to 3 cloves garlic (minced or pressed) and 2 T. minced parsley; beat until fluffy. Cover and refrigerate until ready to use.

LEMON BUTTER AUX FINES HERBES: Combine ½ C. (1/4 lb) butter (at room temperature), 1 T. each of minced parsley and chopped chives (fresh or frozen or freeze dried), 2 t. lemon juice, ½ t. each of tarragon and chervil leaves. ¼ t. salt and a dash of pepper – beat until fluffy. Cover and refrigerate until ready to use.

BASIL BUTTER: Combine ½ C. (1/4 lb) butter (at room temperature). ½ C. lightly packed, chopped basil or 2 T. dry basil, ¼ C. grated Parmesan cheese, 2 T. minced parsley and 1 T. lemon juice; beat until fluffy. Cover and refrigerate.

DILL BUTTER: Press yolks of 2 hard cooked eggs through a wire strainer (reserve whites for other use). Combine with ½ C. butter, 3 t. dill weed, ½ t. salt and 1/8 t. pepper; beat until fluffy. Cover and refrigerate.

HOT HERB-LEMON OR NUT BUTTERS

CLASSIC LEMON BUTTER– melt ¼ C. butter over medium heat; add juice of 1 lemon. Heat until butter bubbles, stir lightly.

PARSLEY LEMON BUTTER- Make classic lemon butter as directed in preceding recipe. Add 1 to 2 T. minced parsley along with the lemon juice.

SAGE LEMON BUTTER – Make classic lemon butter as directed preceding, adding ½ t. mace, 1 t. rubbed sage, a dash of pepper and grated peel of 1 lemon along with lemon juice.

NUT BUTTER- Melt ¼ C. butter over medium heat. Add ¼ to ½ C. nuts (use whole pine nuts; or use chopped slivered or sliced almonds, cashews, filberts, macadamia nuts or pecans). Heat until butter bubbles and nuts are lightly browned (about 5 to 10 minutes).

Made in the USA
Charleston, SC
04 December 2013